S0-BXW-720

To the memory of my dear father,
Sheldon Schwartz

Special Thanks to...

Nancy Davis, for her constant encouragement and patiently guiding the style of this book.

Lisa Brazieal and David Van Ness, for their helpful assistance in dealing with thorny layout and design issues.

Emily Glossbrenner, for creating another superb index under less than optimal circumstances.

Cliff Colby and Marjorie Baer, for continuing to be supportive business associates and dear friends.

contents

introduction   xi

what you'll create   x
how this book works   xiv

go to the Web site   xvi
the next step   xvii

1. about databases   1

database features   2
flat-file vs. relational   5

about FileMaker Pro   6
extra bits   8

2. defining fields   9

make a new database   10
create Text fields   11
create the Date field   12
create Number fields   13
about calculations   16

create Calculation fields   17
about the default layout   22
review the field list   23
extra bits   24

3. creating the data entry layout   25

use the wizard   26
about layout tools   29
remove unneeded parts   31
set field widths   32
color the Body part   34
add background blocks   35
add divider bars   37

add a descriptive title   38
place fields and labels   39
add section labels   41
align and format fields   42
set the tab order   44
save layout changes   45
extra bits   46

contents

4. creating the global settings layout   47

duplicate a layout	48	set formatting	53
edit the background	49	arrange the fields	55
replace the fields	51	extra bits	58

5. creating the blank forms layout   59

create the layout	60	extra bits	66
add the text	64		

6. creating the monthly totals report   67

create the basic layout	68	format text and fields	78
edit the layout	72	make final adjustments	80
change part colors	75	extra bits	82

7. creating the destination report   83

duplicate the layout	84	create a trip count field	88
group by destination	85	extra bits	90
refine the layout	86		

8. adding buttons, scripts, and value lists   91

create a button	92	define value lists	105
add Data Entry buttons	94	create report scripts	108
label the buttons	95	make a startup script	113
create one-step scripts	96	set the script order	115
create the sort script	97	delete the initial layout	117
create the trip log script	99	extra bits	118
create new record script	102		

contents

9. using the database 121

enter the global data	122	find records	127
delete the test records	123	start a new year	128
create the first record	124	customization tips	129
create more records	125	extra bits	131
use Data Entry buttons	126		

index 133

introduction

The Visual QuickProject Guide that you hold in your hands offers a unique way to learn about new technologies. Instead of drowning you in theoretical possibilities and lengthy explanations, this Visual QuickProject Guide uses big, color illustrations coupled with clear, concise step-by-step instructions to show you how to complete one specific project in a matter of hours.

Our project in this book is to create a simple (but elegant) FileMaker Pro 7 database for recording and reporting business mileage. If you're required—either by the company you work for or by the IRS—to keep a log of mileage driven for business, you'll find this database very useful. But even if tracking business mileage isn't one of your needs, the other purpose of this book is to teach you about FileMaker Pro; that is, you'll learn by doing. By creating the database, you will see how to use FileMaker to create databases that are of interest to you. You'll define fields, set field validation and auto-entry options, create data entry and report layouts, define value lists that will pop-up when you tab or click into certain fields, and automate database functions with scripts and clickable buttons.

Different platforms. Most of the screen shots in this book were taken on a Mac running OS X. However, FileMaker Pro is a cross-platform product. If you're a Windows user, you'll find that the dialog boxes you see onscreen are similar to the Mac ones shown here. In the rare instance where there's an important difference between the platforms, I'll point it out. For example, keyboard shortcuts used by the two are different. Whenever a keyboard shortcut is included in this book, it will be presented in Mac/Windows order, such as ⌘C/Ctrl C.

what you'll create

We'll start by defining the fields used in the database, specifying a field type for each one, as well as options (validation criteria and auto-entry values).

You create and edit field definitions on the Fields tab of the Define Database window.

Clickable buttons automate common tasks

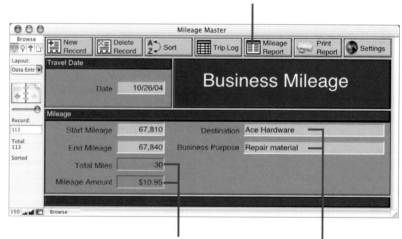

You'll create this Data Entry layout and use it to record your trips.

Calculated fields compute the mileage and monetary value of each trip

Pop-up value lists for these fields help ensure that consistent data is entered

You'll create a Global Settings layout on which you'll enter all the constants that are used in calculations, such as your odometer reading on January 1 and the amount allowed (per mile) by the IRS for business mileage. This layout also displays a running total for your business miles and their dollar value.

Constants

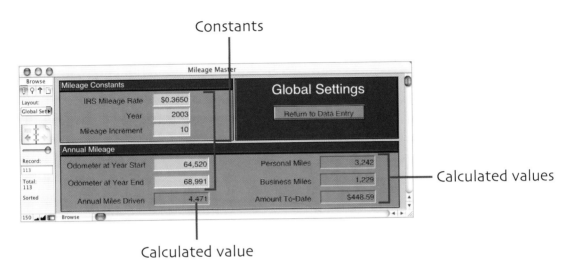

Calculated values

Calculated value

You'll create a script-controlled report that you can view onscreen or print. To generate this year-to-date monthly summary, all you'll have to do is click the Mileage Report button on the Data Entry layout.

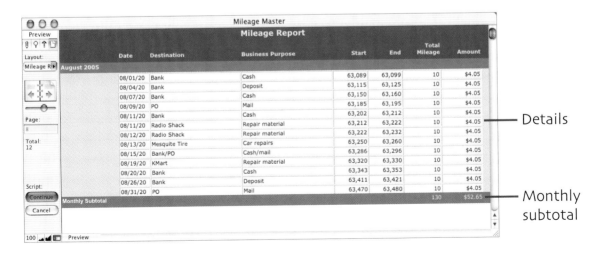

Details

Monthly subtotal

what you'll create (cont.)

Destination Report is a variation of the Mileage Report and is also generated by a script you'll create. Instead of monthly totals, the Destination Report generates a separate total for each destination. To create the onscreen or printed version of this report, you'll select a command from the Scripts menu.

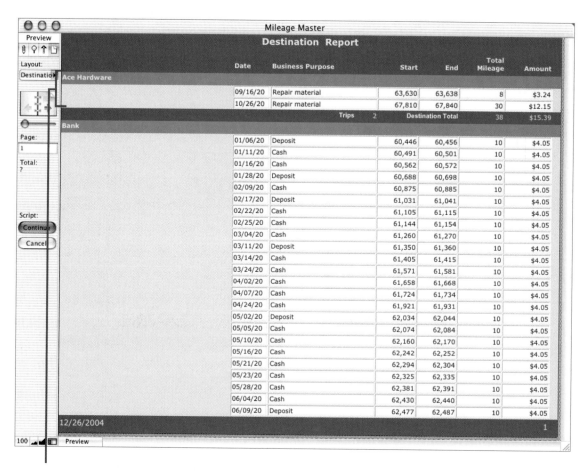

A separate report section is generated for each destination.

The Blank Form layout is simply a form you'll print to create a monthly trip log for your vehicle. You'll use it to record the details of each trip and then transfer the data to the database when it's convenient.

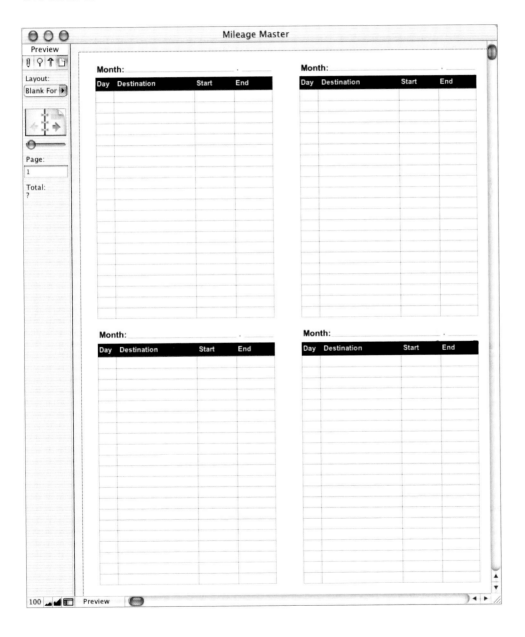

how this book works

Each section begins with a descriptive title.

Callout text explains screen shot elements.

Procedures that you must perform in order are presented as numbered steps.

Key terms and items you must type or choose are displayed as orange text.

Illustrative screen shots show what you'll see on your monitor or what you need to do.

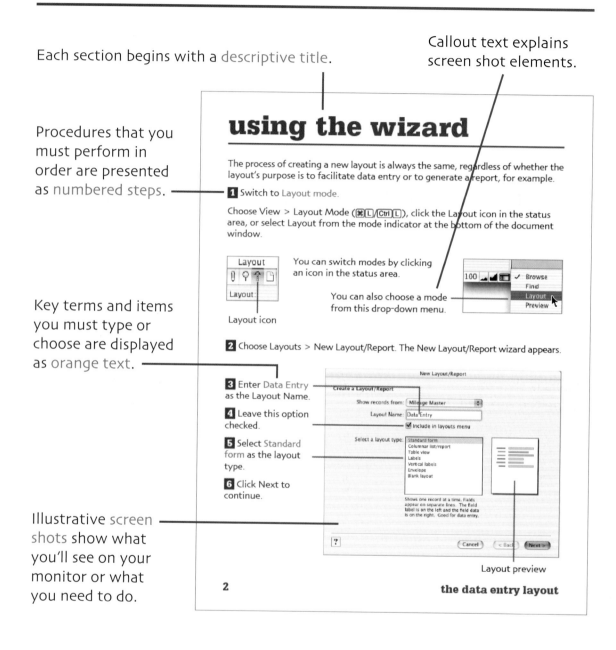

using the wizard

The process of creating a new layout is always the same, regardless of whether the layout's purpose is to facilitate data entry or to generate a report, for example.

1 Switch to Layout mode.

Choose View > Layout Mode (⌘L/Ctrl L), click the Layout icon in the status area, or select Layout from the mode indicator at the bottom of the document window.

Layout
⋮ ♀ ⬚ ▯
Layout:

Layout icon

You can switch modes by clicking an icon in the status area.

You can also choose a mode from this drop-down menu.

100 ◢▗▙▐ ✓ Browse
Find
Layout
Preview

2 Choose Layouts > New Layout/Report. The New Layout/Report wizard appears.

3 Enter Data Entry as the Layout Name.

4 Leave this option checked.

5 Select Standard form as the layout type.

6 Click Next to continue.

New Layout/Report

Create a Layout/Report

Show records from: Mileage Master

Layout Name: Data Entry

☑ Include in layouts menu

Select a layout type: Standard form
Columnar list/report
Table view
Labels
Vertical labels
Envelope
Blank layout

Shows one record at a time. Fields appear on separate lines. The field label is on the left and the field data is on the right. Good for data entry.

[?] Cancel   < Back   Next >

Layout preview

the data entry layout

2

An extra bits section at the end of each chapter contains tips and tricks you might like to know—but that aren't absolutely necessary for creating the database.

The heading for each group of tips matches the section title.

The page number on which the section begins is shown beside the heading.

Each chapter section referred to in Extra Bits is indicated by a different colored block.

extra bits

use the wizard p. 26

- If you want to create a layout from scratch (instead of using one of FileMaker's colorful layout themes), choose Blank Layout in the New Layout/Report wizard.
- As you'll learn in later chapters, there will be layouts that you may not want to list in the layouts menu (found above the status area). For example, you may want to prevent users from switching directly to a report layout because it wouldn't show the proper information in Browse mode.

about layout tools p. 29

- While we'll be using the Size palette to measure distances and sizes in inches, you can also use two other measurements systems. Click the measurement unit to the right of any Size palette text box to change the units to centimeters or pixels.

remove unneeded parts p. 31

- The Part Setup dialog box is also used to add parts. Later in the book, we'll use it that way to add Subsummary parts to a report.

set field widths p. 32

- The object dimensions and locations in this chapter aren't sacred. Neither are the fonts or font sizes. The size and format of items is up to you. If you think you can improve the layout, feel free to experiment.

place fields and labels p. 39

- There are several ways to precisely align a group of fields, labels, or graphics. You can drag them to the same grid location (when object grids is enabled), set the same position on the Size palette, or choose the Arrange > Align or Set Alignment command.
- To make small adjustments to the position of a selected object, press the appropriate arrow key. This is referred to as nudging. Even with object grids enabled, you can use this technique to override the normal "snap to grid" behavior.
- If you make a mistake, immediately choose Edit > Undo. If you cannot correct a layout error this way, you can revert to the last saved version by choosing Don't Save when offered the chance to save changes.

46   creating the data entry layout

go to the Web site

Some of the graphic elements used in this database are very time-consuming to construct. To save yourself some unnecessary work, you can download them from my Web site at: www.siliconwasteland.com/fmp.htm

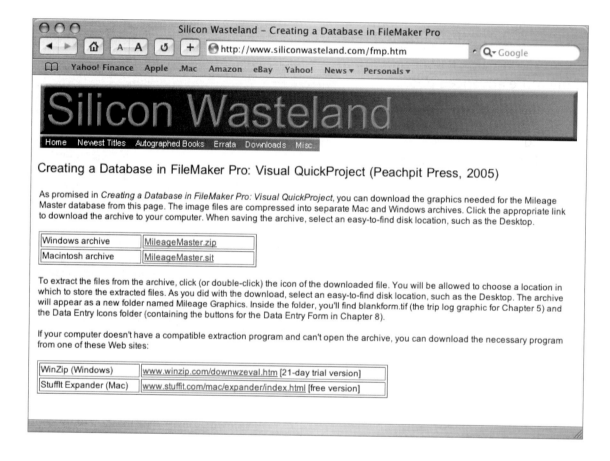

the next step

Working through the material in this book will teach you many of the skills needed to become familiar with FileMaker Pro. But there's a lot more for you to learn. When you're ready to continue your education, pick up a copy of my more advanced book: FileMaker Pro 7 Bible. Regardless of your FileMaker skill level, you'll find this 900-page reference both informative and helpful.

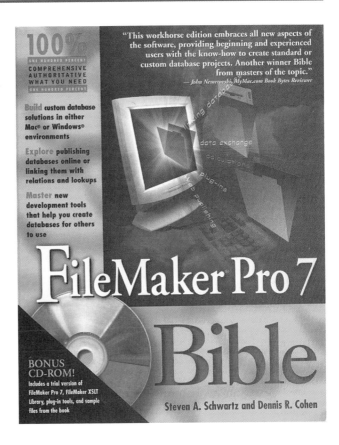

100%
ONE HUNDRED PERCENT
COMPREHENSIVE
AUTHORITATIVE
WHAT YOU NEED
ONE HUNDRED PERCENT

Build custom database solutions in either Mac® or Windows® environments

Explore publishing databases online or linking them with relations and lookups

Master new development tools that help you create databases for others to use

"This workhorse edition embraces all new aspects of the software, providing beginning and experienced users with the know-how to create standard or custom database projects. Another winner Bible from masters of the topic."
— John Nemerovski, MyMac.com Book Bytes Reviewer

FileMaker Pro 7
Bible

BONUS CD-ROM!
Includes a trial version of FileMaker Pro 7, FileMaker XSLT Library, plug-in tools, and sample files from the book

Steven A. Schwartz and Dennis R. Cohen

1. about databases

If you're new to databases or just new to FileMaker Pro, you'll need some background information before you're ready to create the database (Mileage Master) that's the subject of this book. This chapter will help bring you up to speed on databases in general and FileMaker Pro in particular.

A computer database is an organized collection of information on a specific topic. Databases can be created for home (recipe collections, greeting card lists, bowling league records), school (contacts, assignments, software registrations), and business (inventory tracking, invoices, petty cash disbursements). A complete set of data for one employee, recipe, team member, or invoice is called a record; the data elements within a record are called fields. Every field collects a single, discrete piece of information, such as a person's last name, the quantity of an item in a recipe, or an employee's Social Security number.

You enter data into the fields you've defined.

In this database, every record contains the data you've entered for one medical incident. Fields store a date of service, service type, description, charge, and so on.

Some fields, such as Net Expense, are calculated for you, using a formula that combines the contents of other fields.

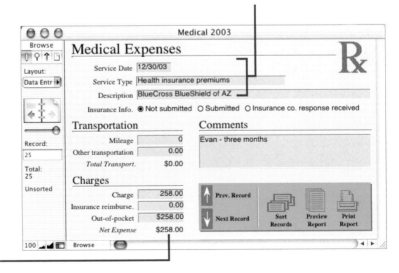

1

database features

If all you could do with a database was enter and flip through records, it would be no more useful than a stack of index cards. But databases also provide many capabilities to help you organize, view, find, and analyze your data.

Sorting. People seldom want to view their data in the order in which it was entered. Instead, you can sort a database by one or several fields, putting it in exactly the order you need at the moment—whether because you want to flip through records in the new order or need to create an impressive report.

Last	First	Zip Code
Jones	Marcia	01990
Jones	Kenneth	23906
Jones	Andrea	66211
Smith	Donald	45791
Zimmerman	Louis	77429

Sorting on the Last field arranges everyone by their last name. But people with the same last name aren't in any particular order.

Last	First	Zip Code
Jones	Andrea	66211
Jones	Kenneth	23906
Jones	Marcia	01990
Smith	Donald	45791
Zimmerman	Louis	77429

Sorting on the Last and First fields still puts people with the same last name together, but arranges them in a useful order. Last names that are the same are further sorted by first name.

Finding records. Every database program has a command or procedure for identifying records that match one or several criteria. You can use it to find a specific record (Jay Smith) or a subset of records (mint stamps with a catalog value of more than $100).

Mint Value	Used Value
>100	

Data validation. A database is only as good as its data. To prevent unacceptable data from being entered, you can set validation criteria for fields. You can specify that only numbers be entered in a Cost field, for example. Or you can insist that every person's age be greater than or equal to 18, or that only Zip Codes between 01704 and 01718 will be allowed.

Calculations. You can create fields that perform simple or complex calculations within each record to compute the total for an invoice, the number of days until a report is due, or the exact length of a phone call based on its starting and ending times. Database programs also provide built-in functions that you can use to perform calculations, such as statistics, business math, extracting characters from text strings, and converting from one data type to another.

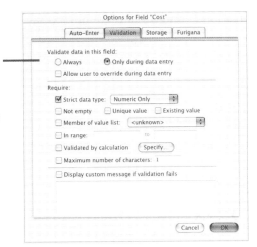

Purchase Price / Mint Value

Scripts. To enable you to quickly and accurately perform repetitive, multi-step tasks, most database programs allow you to create scripts or macros. A script can perform a task as simple as switching to a Help layout or as complex as selecting a subset of records, sorting the database, printing the resulting report, and then restoring the data to its original order. The manner in which scripts are executed varies from one program to another.

```
✦  Enter Browse Mode []
✦  Go to Layout ["Data Entry"]
✦  Print Setup [Restore; No dialog]
✦  Sort Records [Restore; No dialog]
✦  Go to Record/Request/Page [First]
```

This FileMaker script switches to the Data Entry layout, sorts the database, and then displays the first record.

database features (cont.)

Reports. One of the most important features of a database is the ability to generate reports. A custom report can be based on all or only selected data, include category groupings, and display a variety of summary statistics, such as counts, averages, subtotals, running totals, and grand totals.

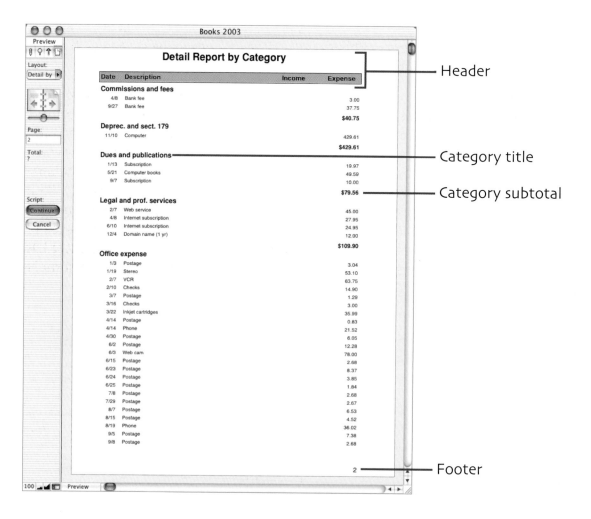

about databases

flat-file vs. relational

You can build two types of databases in most modern database programs: flat file and relational. In a flat-file database, all necessary fields are defined in a single file or table. A relational database, on the other hand, is composed of multiple files or tables, related to one another by matching key fields in the files or tables. The main advantage of a relational database is that it avoids unnecessary data duplication. Rather than retyping the same information in every record that requires it (such as a student's address), the data can simply be displayed by referencing the table in which it's stored.

For example, an invoicing database might have three tables: Invoices, Customers, and Products. A relationship could be defined between Invoices and the Customers table, based on a Customer ID field. Another relationship could be defined between Invoices and Products, based on a Product ID field. When you create a new invoice and enter a Customer ID, the matching ID in the Customers table is found, enabling the customer's address information to instantly be displayed in the invoice. When you enter a Product ID, the Products table is consulted and the information for that item is displayed. If you have repeat customers and products that you sell to many people, you'll save an enormous amount of time by only having to enter IDs in each invoice—rather than retyping data that's already stored in the Customers and Products tables.

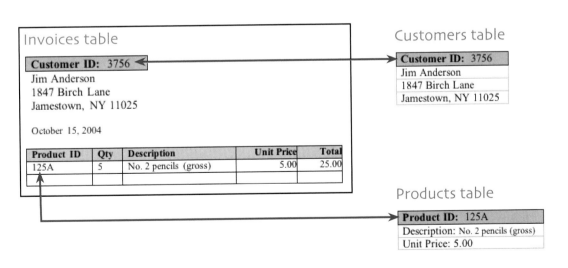

about FileMaker Pro

FileMaker Pro is a mode-oriented program. Almost everything you do requires that you be in the proper mode: Browse, Find, Layout, or Preview. (Note, however, that a few operations, such as creating or changing field definitions or value lists, can be performed in several modes.)

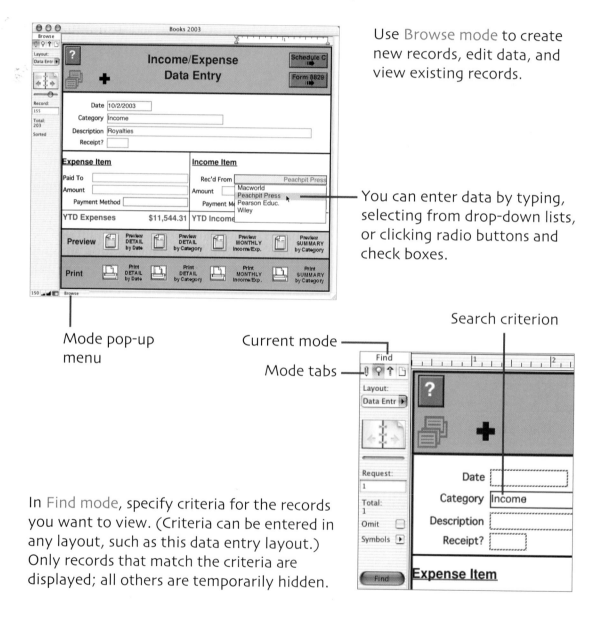

Use Browse mode to create new records, edit data, and view existing records.

You can enter data by typing, selecting from drop-down lists, or clicking radio buttons and check boxes.

Mode pop-up menu

Current mode

Mode tabs

Search criterion

In Find mode, specify criteria for the records you want to view. (Criteria can be entered in any layout, such as this data entry layout.) Only records that match the criteria are displayed; all others are temporarily hidden.

A FileMaker layout is an arrangement of selected fields, field labels, and objects. You can create as many layouts as you need; each for a specific purpose, such as entering data, displaying a report, or printing labels.

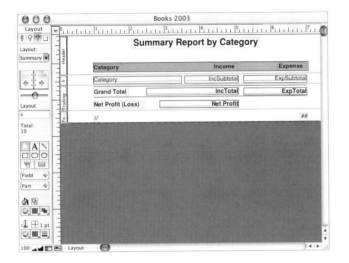

When printed or viewed in Preview mode, this layout will generate the report below.

Layout mode

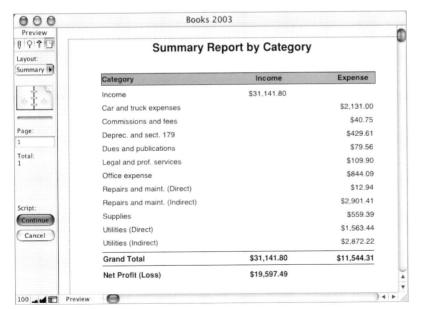

Preview mode

extra bits

database features p. 2

- In addition to setting a single Find criterion, you can specify multiple criteria. You can search for records that satisfy any of the criteria (an Or search) or records that satisfy all of the criteria (an And search).

- You can also perform a Find that locates records within a range, such as all people between the ages of 18 and 21.

- In FileMaker Pro, scripts can be executed by choosing the script name from the Scripts menu or by clicking a button to which the script has been attached.

flat-file vs. relational p. 5

- Conceptually, flat-file databases are much easier for new users to understand. While more powerful and flexible, learning to create relational databases has a much steeper learning curve.

about FileMaker Pro p. 6

- A FileMaker layout can include as many or as few of the defined fields as you like. Think of a layout as simply one view into the database.

- There is no requirement that a field be included in any of a database's layouts. Some fields are intended only as a part of a calculation, for example.

- The addition of simple scripts— often only a single step—can greatly enhance a database's ease of use. For example, you can create one-step scripts to change to a particular layout, create a new record, delete the current record, or restore the database to a default sort order.

- Any FileMaker database can also have a when opening or when closing script that automatically runs each time the database is opened or closed.

about databases

2. defining fields

Creating a database from scratch (rather than copying an existing one or using a template) involves many steps, but the first is always to define its fields. Although you don't have to immediately define every field—FileMaker is perfectly happy if you add, delete, and edit field definitions as you develop and refine the database—I'll make it easy for you. Since I already know what fields will be needed, we'll create and set options for all of them in this chapter.

Some fields will be used for gathering data, others for performing calculations, and still others for presenting reports. After naming and specifying a type for each field (such as Text, Number, or Calculation), we'll set options for the fields. Field options can be divided into the following classes:

Auto-enter. These options let you specify a default value that will automatically be entered for the field whenever you create a new record. An auto-enter value could be the next serial number in a sequence, today's date, or a fixed value (such as California or 100.00).

Validation. Validation settings are used to prevent unwanted values in a field. For example, you can specify that a field's value be within a particular range, that the value be unique, or that its length be limited to a maximum number of characters. You can also specify whether a user will be allowed to override the validation criteria.

Storage. You can set storage options to index a field (allowing you to rapidly sort on or search the field) or treat it as a global field (giving it a single value for the entire database, as you might do to set a sales tax percentage).

After we finish defining fields and setting options for them, FileMaker will generate a default layout for the database.

make a new database

1 New databases are created in the New Database dialog box. If you've just launched FileMaker Pro, the dialog box will appear automatically. If FileMaker is already running, choose File > New Database to open the dialog box.

2 In the New Database dialog box, select Create a new empty file and then click OK.

3 A file dialog box appears. Name the database Mileage Master.fp7, specify where on disk to store the file, and click the Save button.

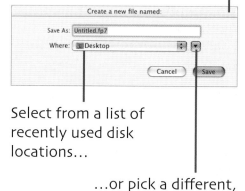

Select from a list of recently used disk locations...

...or pick a different, unlisted location.

4 The Define Database dialog box appears, open to the Fields tab. To create each new field, enter its name, choose a field type, and click Create.

The field list will appear here.

The specific fields you'll create, as well as their field types and options, will be explained on the pages that follow.

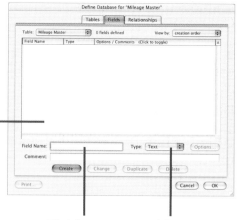

Field name   Field type

create Text fields

At a minimum, a field definition consists of a field name and a type. The field type determines what kind of data will be stored in the field. Of the eight field types supported by FileMaker Pro 7, Mileage Master uses Text, Number, Date, Calculation, and Summary field types. Define each field listed in the following pages by entering the name in the Field Name box, choosing the designated field type from the Type drop-down menu, and clicking Create. To set any options that are indicated for a field, select the field name on the Fields tab of the Define Database dialog box, click Options, and then click the appropriate tab.

Text fields can store any kind of character data, including letters, numbers, and punctuation. Examples of Text fields include addresses, comments, and phone numbers. (Because phone numbers are generally typed using non-numeric characters, such as minuses and parentheses, they are better represented as Text fields than as Number fields.)

Create two Text fields: Destination and Business Purpose. On the Storage tab of the Options dialog box, set Indexing to Minimal, as described below.

1 After defining the two Text fields (as shown on the previous page), select one of them in the field list in the Define Database dialog box, click Options, and click the Storage tab on the Options dialog box.

2 In the Indexing section, click the Minimal radio button. Then click OK to return to the Define Database dialog box.

3 Repeat Steps 1 and 2 for the other Text field.

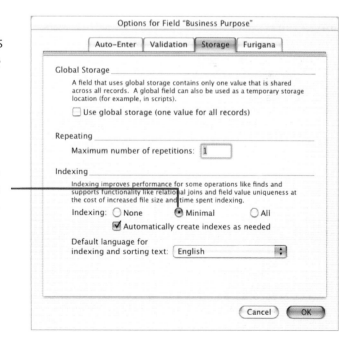

create the Date field

Date fields are used to record dates. Although you could also use a Text field to store dates, only a Date field will sort dates properly, make them readily searchable, and enable you to easily use them in date-based calculations.

Create a single Date field named Date. The field will be used to record the date of each trip. Because we want to be able to rapidly sort the database on this field, go to the Storage tab of the Options dialog box and set Indexing to All. We'll also set the default value for this field to the date on which each new record is created, as described below.

Auto-Enter tab

1 Select the Date field in the field list in the Define Database dialog box, click Options, and click the Auto-Enter tab on the Options dialog box.

2 Click the Creation check box and choose Date from the drop-down menu beside it.

3 Click OK to return to the Define Database dialog box.

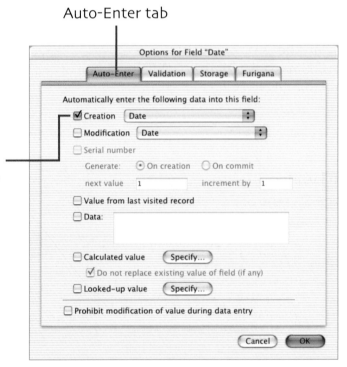

Although the current date will automatically be entered for every new record, you can still edit it if necessary. (Even if the date is incorrect, it will usually be faster for you to edit it than to type it from scratch.)

defining fields

create Number fields

Number fields are used to store numeric data: the digits 0–9, a decimal point, and a sign (+ or -). You use a Number field when you want to be able to sort numerically (rather than alphabetically), perform calculations on the field, or use the data in a Summary field (as a summary calculation in a report, for example).

Only two Number fields in this database will have to be entered for each record. They are the beginning and ending mileage for each trip (Start Mileage and End Mileage). All other Number fields are global; that is, each will have one value for the entire database and will be used as a constant in calculations.

We'll start by creating the five global Number fields: Mileage Rate, Start Yr, End Yr, Year, and Mileage Increment.

1 In the Define Database dialog box, create the Mileage Rate field by entering its name in the Field Name box, choosing Number from the Type drop-down menu, and clicking Create.

———————————————————— Number field type

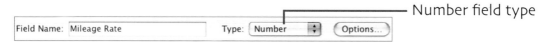

2 With the new Number field selected in the field list, click Options, and click the Storage tab on the Options dialog box.

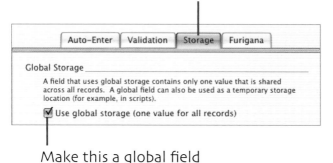

3 Click the check box in the Global Storage section. Then click OK to return to the Define Database dialog box.

Make this a global field

4 Repeat these steps for the other four global Number fields: Start Yr, End Yr, Year, and Mileage Increment.

create Number fields (cont.)

Start Mileage and End Mileage are also Number fields. You'll use them to record the odometer readings for the start and end of each trip.

1 In the Define Database dialog box, create the Start Mileage field by entering its name in the Field Name box, choosing Number from the Type drop-down menu, and clicking Create.

2 Click Options, and then click the Storage tab on the Options dialog box. Set Indexing to All.

3 Click the Validation tab. In the Validate data in this field section, click Always to specify when data will be evaluated. Remove the check mark from Allow user to override during data entry.

4 In the Require section, click the Strict data type check box and choose Numeric Only from the drop-down menu. Click OK to return to the Define Database dialog box. (These validation options specify that only numbers will be accepted in the field.)

5 To create the End Mileage field, perform Steps 1–7, but skip Step 2. (The default indexing setting of Automatically create indexes as needed will suffice.)

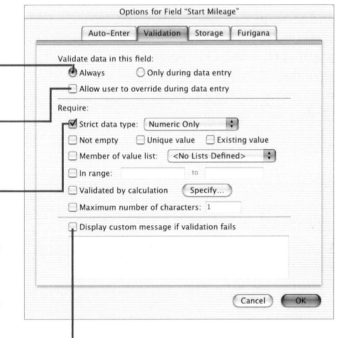

6 Click the Display custom message if validation fails check box and enter this text in the box below it: The value for End Mileage must be larger than the value for Start Mileage. This message will appear if you mistakenly enter an End Mileage that is smaller than the Start Mileage. You must then correct your error.

7 To determine if an End Mileage value is correct, it is validated by calculation. When you commit (complete) a record, a check is made to see if End Mileage is greater than or equal to Start Mileage. If it isn't, the error message from Step 6 is displayed.

To create the validation formula, click the Validated by calculation check box. In the Specify Calculation dialog box that appears, enter this formula:

End Mileage ≥ Start Mileage

You create formulas by typing and/or selecting elements (field names, operators, and built-in functions) from the top half of the dialog box. (At a minimum, it's safest to select field names by double-clicking them in the field list. Doing so ensures that they're spelled correctly.) When you've completed the formula, click OK. Then click OK again to dismiss the Options dialog box, returning you to the Define Database dialog box.

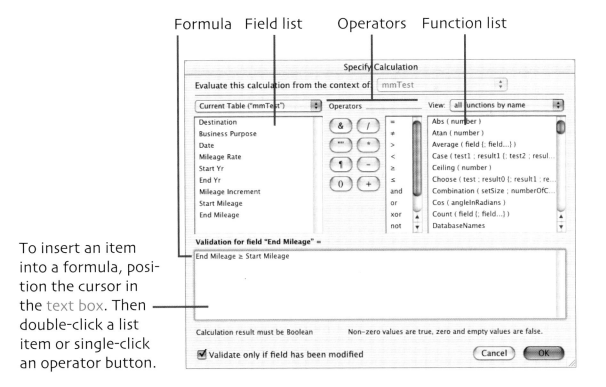

Formula   Field list   Operators   Function list

To insert an item into a formula, position the cursor in the text box. Then double-click a list item or single-click an operator button.

about calculations

FileMaker Pro allows you to perform two kinds of calculations: within records and across records. Each is handled by a different field type.

Within-record calculations are accomplished using Calculation fields. A formula may combine other fields, constants, and built-in functions. For example, you could create a Calculation field that computes sales tax by multiplying an invoice total by a sales tax percentage (Invoice Total * Tax Percent) or by a constant (Invoice Total * .075). The computed sales tax would be different for each invoice. Calculations can be performed on Number, Text, Date, Time, or Container fields; the specified result must also be one of these data types. If you change the data in any field on which a calculation is based, the result is automatically recalculated. Unlike other field types, the result in a Calculation field cannot be edited. (You can copy the result, but you can't change it.)

Calculations that are computed across all or a subset of records in the database are performed using Summary fields. Although Summary fields can be placed in data entry layouts, it's more common to use them in reports.

As shown in the tables below, Mileage Master has six Calculation fields and two Summary fields. You'll note that formulas in a few Calculation fields rely on Summary fields and vice versa. Thus, some fields must be created before others.

Calculation Field	Formula	Result Type	Storage Opt.
Total Mileage	End Mileage - Start Mileage	Number	
Mileage Amount	Total Mileage * Mileage Rate	Number	Unstored
Annual Miles	If(not(IsEmpty(End Yr)); End Yr - Start Yr; "")	Number	Global
Month	MonthName(Date)	Text	
Personal Miles	If(not(IsEmpty(Annual Miles)); Annual Miles - MilesSum; "")	Number	Global
Annual Dollar	Mileage Rate * MilesSum	Number	Global

Summary Field	Function and Summarized Field
MilesSum	Total of Total Mileage
MilesExpSum	Total of Mileage Amount

create Calculation fields

Total Mileage. This Calculation field computes the number of miles for each trip.

1 In the Define Database dialog box, enter Total Mileage in the Field Name box, choose Calculation as the Type, and click Create. The Specify Calculation dialog box appears.

2 Create the formula. Double-click the End Mileage field in the field list, type a minus sign (-), and then double-click the Start Mileage field.

Field list ——

Formula ——

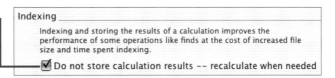

3 Set the result type to Number, and then click OK.

Mileage Amount. This Calculation field computes the dollar amount for each trip by multiplying the miles traveled (Total Mileage) by the Mileage Rate (a constant).

1 Create this Calculation field as you did Total Mileage. But in the Specify Calculation dialog box, use this formula: Total Mileage * Mileage Rate

2 Set the result type to Number, and then click the Storage Options button.

3 Ensure that Indexing is set to Do not store calculation results, click OK, and then click OK again to return to the Define Database dialog box.

Indexing

Indexing and storing the results of a calculation improves the performance of some operations like finds at the cost of increased file size and time spent indexing.

☑ Do not store calculation results -- recalculate when needed

create Calculation fields

Month. This Calculation field extracts the name of the month from each trip's date (10/14/05 yields October, for example). This data is used in section heads of the Mileage Report when displaying monthly trip totals.

1 Create a Calculation field named Month. The Specify Calculation dialog box appears when you click Create.

2 Insert the MonthName function into the formula by double-clicking its name in the function list.

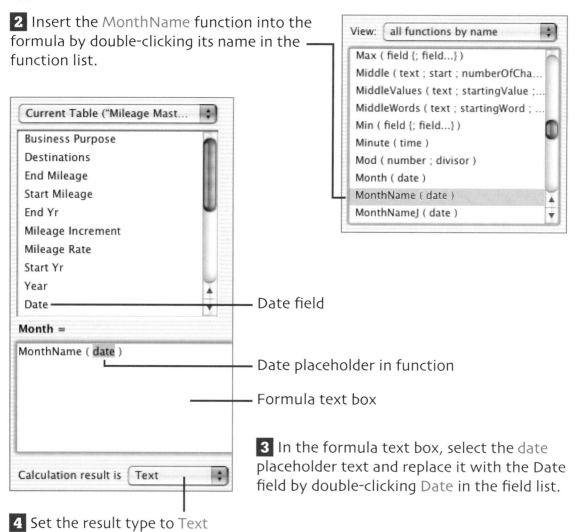

Date field

Date placeholder in function

Formula text box

3 In the formula text box, select the date placeholder text and replace it with the Date field by double-clicking Date in the field list.

4 Set the result type to Text and then click OK.

defining fields

MilesSum and MilesExpSum. Since the Calculation fields on which these Summary fields are based have been defined, we can create them now. MilesSum computes the total miles traveled each month and the grand total of all miles traveled to-date. MilesExpSum computes the dollar value for the miles traveled each month and the total dollar value of all miles traveled to-date.

1 Create a Summary field named MilesSum. When you click Create, the Options for Summary Field "MilesSum" dialog box appears.

2 Click the Total of radio button, select Total Mileage in the Available Fields list, and click OK to return to the Define Database dialog box.

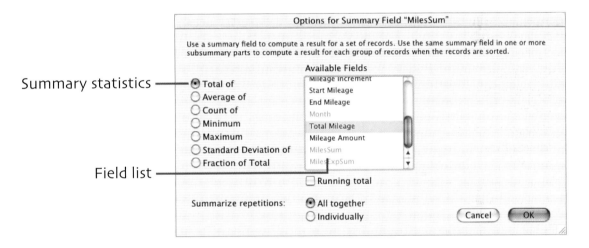

1 Now create the MilesExpSum Summary field. When you click Create, the Options for Summary Field "MilesExpSum" dialog box appears.

2 Click the Total of radio button, select Mileage Amount in the Available Fields list, and click OK to return to the Define Database dialog box.

create Calculation fields

Annual Dollar. This global Calculation field computes the dollar value of the business miles driven during the year by multiplying the IRS' Mileage Rate by MilesSum, the total miles for the year.

1 In the Define Database dialog box, type Annual Dollar in the Field Name box, choose Calculation as the Type, and click Create. The Specify Calculation dialog box appears.

2 Create the formula by double-clicking the Mileage Rate field in the field list, typing an asterisk (*), and then double-clicking the MilesSum field.

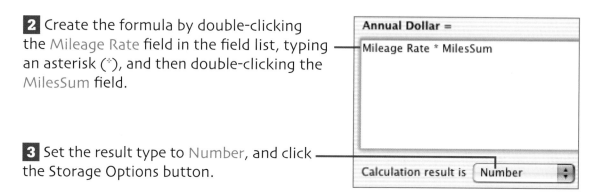

Annual Dollar =

Mileage Rate * MilesSum

3 Set the result type to Number, and click the Storage Options button.

Calculation result is [Number]

4 In the Storage Options dialog box, click the Use global storage (one value for all records) check box. Click OK to dismiss the dialog box, and click OK again to close the Specify Calculation dialog box.

Annual Miles and Personal Miles. Each of these global Calculation fields computes a single value for the entire database: total miles driven during the year (Annual Miles) and the number of non-business miles driven for the year (Personal Miles). Both fields will be displayed on the Global Settings screen, but only at year end—after you've entered the final odometer reading for the year.

1 In the Define Database dialog box, type Annual Miles in the Field Name box, choose Calculation as the Type, and click Create.

2 In the Specify Calculation dialog box, create the following formula:

If (not (IsEmpty (End Yr)); End Yr - Start Yr; "")

Here's what the formula means. If End Yr (final odometer reading) isn't blank, subtract Start Yr (the beginning reading) from End Yr. This yields the total miles driven for the year. Otherwise, leave it blank (the two double quotation marks).

3 Set the result type to Number, and click the Storage Options button.

4 In the Storage Options dialog box, click the Use global storage (one value for all records) check box. Click OK to dismiss the dialog box, and click OK again to close the Specify Calculation dialog box.

Personal Miles. To create this global Calculation field, follow the steps you used to create Annual Miles, but use this formula in Step 2:

If (not (IsEmpty (Annual Miles)); Annual Miles - MilesSum; "")

If Annual Miles (total miles for the year) is not blank, business miles (MilesSum) are subtracted from Annual Miles. This yields the personal miles driven for the year. Otherwise, the field is left blank (represented by the pair of double quotation marks).

Now you've defined the essential fields for the Mileage Master database. One more will be added in a later chapter, but these are all we'll need for now.

about the default layout

Now that the fields have been defined, click OK to close the Define Database dialog box. FileMaker generates a default layout for the database, placing all the defined fields in a single vertical column. The field names are used as labels for the fields. If all you wanted was a quick-and-dirty database, you could start entering data immediately. Or you could clean up the layout slightly by rearranging fields, removing unnecessary ones, and editing labels to make them more descriptive.

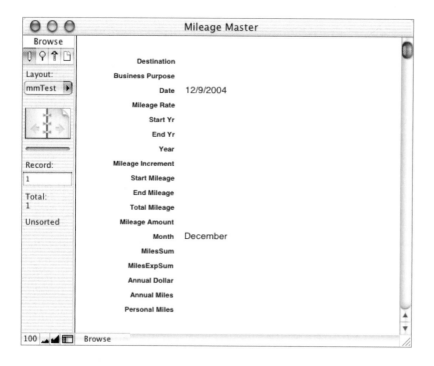

The default layout is only a starting place for most databases. Since all the fields you just defined are used, many (such as the Summary fields) are better removed and placed on other layouts, for example.

Mileage Master, however, is meant to be an example of an attractive, easy to use, highly functional database. Rather than use the default layout (either as-is or after some editing), we can create custom layouts that better serve our needs. As explained in Chapter 1, you can make as many layouts as you like, each for a different purpose. We'll create these custom layouts in the chapters that follow.

review the field list

Compare your field list to the one shown below. (If there are errors in the field names, types, or options, it will affect the way the database works.) Don't worry about the order of the fields, but be sure to check the type and options for each field. You may also want to recheck the result type for the Calculation fields. To do so, double-click each Calculation field in the field list.

extra bits

make a new database p. 10

- When naming and saving a new database, the Windows and Mac file dialog boxes are different. Other dialog boxes may also be slightly different, although they will normally contain the same options.

- It's only critical to include the .fp7 file extension if you're a Windows user. (Note that if you're using FileMaker Pro 5.0–6.0, the correct extension is .fp5.)

create Text fields p. 11

- Don't worry if you make mistakes while defining fields. To change a field's name or type, select it in the Define Database's field list, make the change, and then click the Change button.

- Similarly, it isn't a problem if you exit the dialog box before you've created all the fields. To return to the Define Database dialog box, choose File > Define Database.

create Number fields p. 13

- Since data in Number fields can be entered using any combination of digits, a decimal, and a sign (+ or -), you're probably wondering why we didn't set a format for any of the fields. It's because formatting is specified as part of a layout— not as part of a field definition. Field formatting is discussed in Chapter 3 and later chapters.

about calculations p. 16

- Because the Personal Miles formula is virtually identical to the one for Annual Miles, you may find it simpler to copy the Annual Miles formula in the Specify Calculation dialog box, paste it into the formula box for Personal Miles, and then replace the fields with the correct ones.

- To replace one field with another, select it in the formula and then double-click the replacement field in the field list.

review the field list p. 23

- My version of the Define Database dialog box is probably larger than the one on your screen. You can enlarge the dialog box by clicking its bottom-right corner and then dragging down and to the right.

3. creating the data entry layout

As explained in Chapter 2, the initial/default layout can sometimes be used as-is for data entry. But if you want the database to be attractive and pleasant to use, it's more common to create custom layouts instead. FileMaker simplifies this task by providing the New Layout/Report wizard.

When you use the wizard to create a layout, you specify the manner in which fields are arranged, select only the specific fields you want to include, and apply attractive formatting (called a theme) to the layout. There's always additional work to do afterward, but the wizard will usually give you a solid start in developing the layout you want.

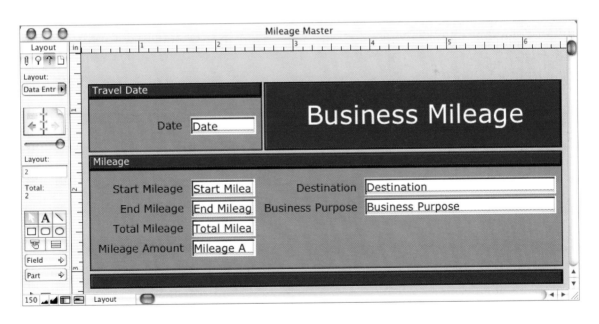

This is what your Data Entry layout will look like by the end of this chapter.

use the wizard

The process of creating a new layout is always the same, regardless of whether the layout's purpose is to facilitate data entry or to generate a report, for example.

1 Switch to Layout mode.

Choose View > Layout Mode (⌘L/Ctrl L), click the Layout icon in the status area, or select Layout from the mode indicator at the bottom of the document window.

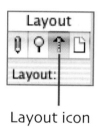

You can switch modes by clicking an icon in the status area.

You can also choose a mode from this drop-down menu.

Layout icon

2 Choose Layouts > New Layout/Report. The New Layout/Report wizard appears.

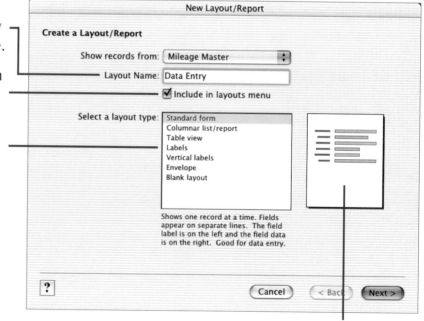

3 Enter Data Entry as the Layout Name.

4 Leave this option checked.

5 Select Standard form as the layout type.

6 Click Next to continue.

Layout preview

creating the data entry layout

On the Specify Fields screen, you select fields for the layout. The order in which fields are selected is the order in which they'll appear on the layout.

Duplicate the Layout fields list shown below by double-clicking a field in the Available fields list to move it into the Layout fields list. If you inadvertently move an incorrect field, select it in the Layout fields list and click Clear. To change the position of a field in the Layout fields list, click the arrow beside its name and drag the field up or down. Click Next when you're done.

Move fields from the Available fields list ...   ... to the Layout fields list.

New Layout/Report

Specify Fields

Specify the fields you want on your layout. Make sure the fields are in the order you want them to appear on your layout.

Available fields

| Current Table ("Mileage ... | ▲▼ |

Destination	
Business Purpose	
Date	
Mileage Rate	
Start Yr	
End Yr	
Year	
Mileage Increment	
Start Mileage	
End Mileage	
Month	
Total Mileage	
Mileage Amount	
MilesSum	
MilesExpSum	

(Clear)

(Move All)

(Clear All)

Layout fields

- ↕ Date
- ↕ Start Mileage
- ↕ End Mileage
- ↕ Total Mileage
- ↕ Mileage Amount
- ↕ Destination
- ↕ Business Purpose

(?)   (Cancel) (< Back) (Next >)

---

creating the data entry layout

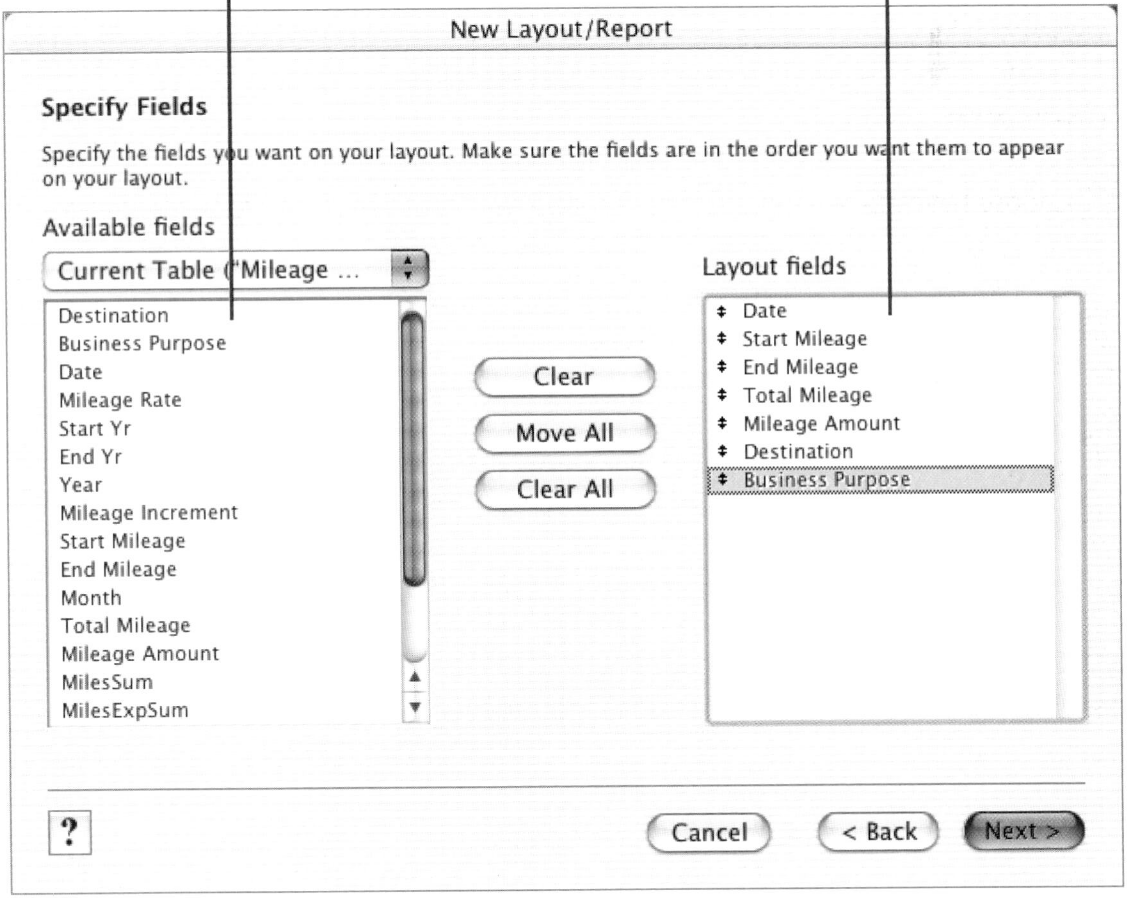

use the wizard (cont.)

On the Select a Theme screen, pick a formatting scheme for the layout. Choose Lavender Screen, and then click the Finish button.

Themes   Preview

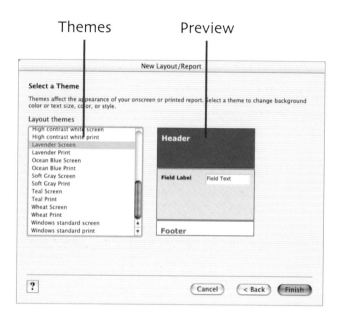

Select a theme based on the purpose of the layout: screen or print. Each layout type is available in many color schemes.

Although the resulting layout is still a single column and only a rough approximation of the final layout, we've saved considerable time by using the wizard. We've placed only the necessary fields and created a uniform appearance for fields and labels.

about layout tools

While some simple layout modifications (such as changing a field or label's size and position) can be accomplished using only the Selection tool, FileMaker includes many other tools that you'll also need to use.

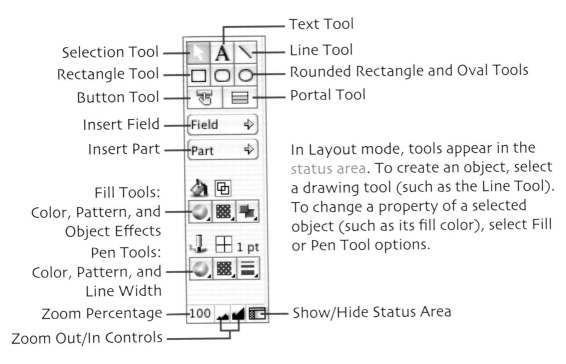

Selection Tool
Rectangle Tool
Button Tool
Insert Field
Insert Part

Text Tool
Line Tool
Rounded Rectangle and Oval Tools
Portal Tool

Fill Tools:
Color, Pattern, and Object Effects
Pen Tools:
Color, Pattern, and Line Width
Zoom Percentage
Zoom Out/In Controls

Show/Hide Status Area

In Layout mode, tools appear in the status area. To create an object, select a drawing tool (such as the Line Tool). To change a property of a selected object (such as its fill color), select Fill or Pen Tool options.

You'll use commands and options on the Text Formatting toolbar (below) to change the formatting of fields, field labels, and static text strings on the layout. If the toolbar isn't visible, choose View > Toolbars > Text Formatting.

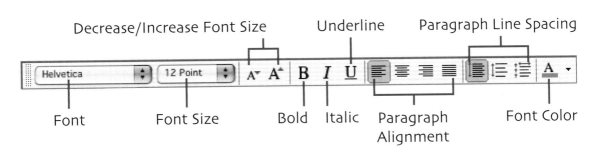

Decrease/Increase Font Size
Underline
Paragraph Line Spacing

Font
Font Size
Bold
Italic
Paragraph Alignment
Font Color

about layout tools (cont.)

You use the Size palette (View > Object Size) to precisely set the size and position of an object. When you select an object, the numbers in the Size palette change to reflect the object's position, width, and height. To change the object's position or size, type a new number into the appropriate box and press ⟨Tab⟩.

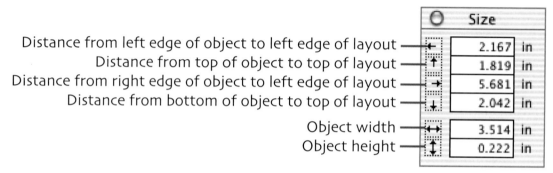

Distance from left edge of object to left edge of layout — 2.167 in
Distance from top of object to top of layout — 1.819 in
Distance from right edge of object to left edge of layout — 5.681 in
Distance from bottom of object to top of layout — 2.042 in

Object width — 3.514 in
Object height — 0.222 in

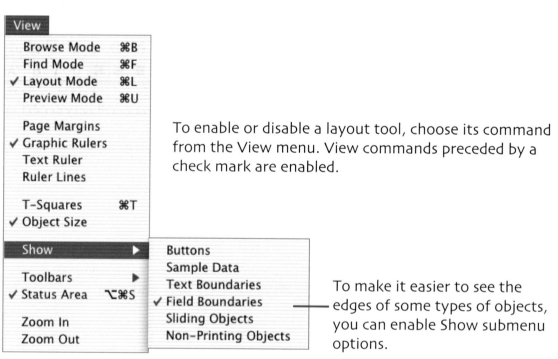

To enable or disable a layout tool, choose its command from the View menu. View commands preceded by a check mark are enabled.

To make it easier to see the edges of some types of objects, you can enable Show submenu options.

creating the data entry layout

remove unneeded parts

As you probably noted, the layout created by the New Layout/Report wizard is divided into three sections (called parts): Header, Body, and Footer. While a Header and Footer are common report parts, we don't need them in a data entry layout. All fields, buttons, and graphic elements can be placed in the Body.

1 Choose Layouts > Part Setup.

2 In the Part Setup dialog box, select the Header part and click Delete.

3 Select the Footer part and click Delete.

4 Click Done. Only the Body remains.

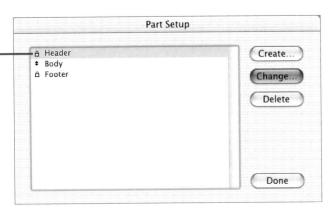

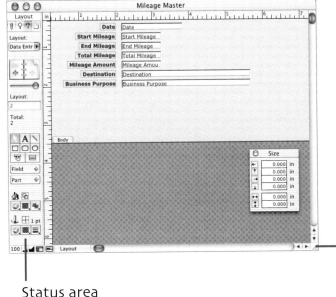

For many of the remaining steps, you'll need to use the tools in the status area. Enlarge the document window so you can see all the tools by dragging the lower-right corner downward.

To change the window size, click here and drag.

Status area

set field widths

The default widths that FileMaker assigns to fields often are not what we want. Field widths can be changed manually by dragging a selection handle or set precisely by entering values in the Size palette.

The Date, Start Mileage, End Mileage, Total Mileage, and Mileage Amount fields will all be the same width: 0.847 inches. The Destination and Business Purpose fields will also be one width, but—since they're intended to hold lengthy text strings—they will be 2.514 inches.

We'll start by manually changing the Date field's width to match the width of the other short fields.

1 Select the Date field by clicking it with the Selection Tool (the pointer).

2 Hold down the (Shift) key, click the Date field's lower-right handle, and drag to the left until the field is the same width as the Start Mileage field below it.

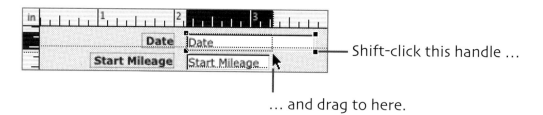

Holding down (Shift) as you drag restricts the size change so it affects only the width or height, depending on the first direction in which you drag.

With object grids enabled (the default setting), when you resize or move an object, it snaps to the nearest grid point—as it did when you resized the Date field. If you've disabled the grids, you can enable them by choosing Arrange > Object Grids.

creating the data entry layout

Now that the smaller fields are the same width, we can simultaneously set them all to the final width using the Size palette (choose View > Object Size).

1 Select the five fields (Date, Start Mileage, End Mileage, Total Mileage, and Mileage Amount) by Shift-clicking each of them or by dragging a selection rectangle around them. (All five fields should now have handles around them.)

2 Enter 0.847 in the Width box of the Size palette and then press Tab.

Repeat this process with the Destination and Business Purpose fields, but set their width to 2.514 inches.

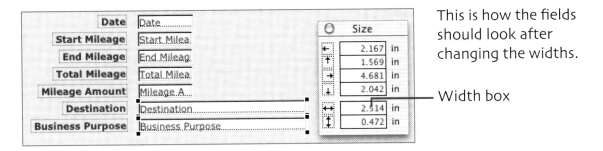

This is how the fields should look after changing the widths.

— Width box

color the Body part

To color an object, you select it and then pick a color and/or pattern from the palettes in the Fill section of the status area. In addition to coloring objects, you can also color an entire part. This creates a solid background for that layout part.

In the current layout, the Body part is already colored a very light purple. We'll make it a solid light purple by changing its fill pattern.

1 On the layout, click the Body tab to select it as the part to be colored.

2 Click the Fill Pattern icon. When the palette appears, click the solid fill icon. The palette closes and the new pattern is applied to the Body.

3 Click anywhere in the Body to deselect the Body tab.

Fill Pattern   Solid fill   Current fill

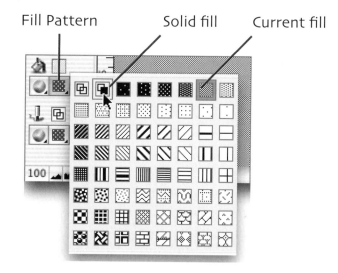

add background blocks

To make the layout more appealing, we'll add some graphic background elements (colored boxes and bars) to break the fields into logical groups. Because it's easier to do this when the fields aren't in the way, we'll start by dragging them off to the side.

1 Widen the layout so there's room to move the labels and fields.

2 Select all the labels and fields by choosing Edit > Select All (⌘A/Ctrl A).

3 While you can now move all the items by dragging, it's easier to do so after grouping them. Choose Arrange > Group (⌘R/Ctrl R). A single set of handles appears around the group.

4 Drag the group to the right, beyond the page break indicator. Click any blank spot in the Body to deselect the group.

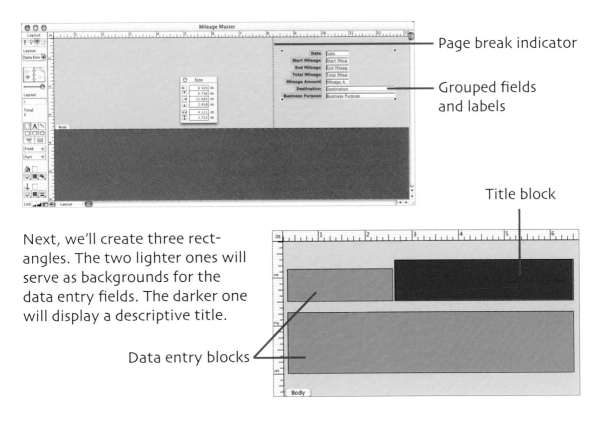

Page break indicator

Grouped fields and labels

Title block

Next, we'll create three rect-angles. The two lighter ones will serve as backgrounds for the data entry fields. The darker one will display a descriptive title.

Data entry blocks

add background blocks

Create the blocks using the fill colors shown below. If your Fill Color palette displays a different set of colors, choose FileMaker Pro > Preferences (Mac) or Edit > Preferences (Windows). In the Preferences dialog box, click the Layout tab and select the System subset (88 colors) palette.

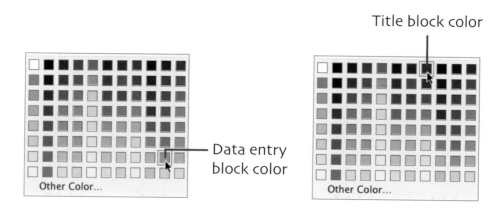

Title block color

Data entry block color

Other Color...

Other Color...

1 To create the small data entry block, select its color from the Fill Color palette and then select the Rectangle Tool. Click the location where the block's upper-left corner will begin, drag down and to the right, and release the mouse button when you're done. (For now, don't worry about the block's exact position or size.)

2 To draw the larger data entry block, select the Rectangle Tool again and draw. Then click any blank spot on the layout to deselect the block.

3 To create the title block, select the indicated color, choose Embossed from the Fill Effects drop-down menu, select the Rectangle Tool, and click and drag.

4 To set the size and position of each block, select a block and enter numbers from the table below into the Size palette. (All table numbers are in inches.)

Block Description	Width	Height	Dist. from Left	Dist. from Top
Small data entry	2.264	0.681	0.333	0.819
Large data entry	6.181	1.278	0.333	1.722
Title	3.889	0.861	2.625	0.639

creating the data entry layout

add divider bars

To further spruce up the layout, we'll add some 3-D bars as element dividers.

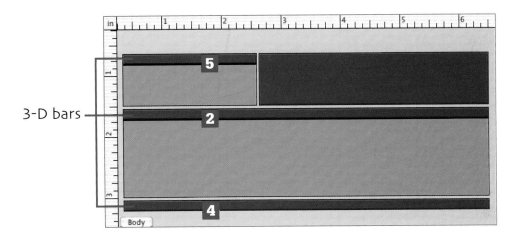

3-D bars

1 Ensure that no element is currently selected. Select the same deep blue color that you used for the title block, choose Embossed as the Fill Effect, ensure that black and 1 pt. (the default settings) are selected for the line color and line width, and select the Rectangle Tool.

2 Draw a bar at the top of the large data block, making it the same width as the data block.

3 Use the Size palette to set the width of the bar to 6.181 inches and the height to 0.181 inches. To align the bar with the top of the large data block, set the left edge distance to 0.333 inches and the top edge to 1.542 inches.

4 This bar will also appear at the bottom of the layout. Select it and choose Edit > Duplicate. Drag the copy so it is slightly below the large data block. (Set the left edge distance to 0.333 inches and top edge to 3.042 inches.)

5 A shorter copy of this bar will be placed at the top of the small data block. Duplicate the upper bar. Set the copy's width to 2.264 inches and drag it into position above the small data block. (Set the left edge distance to 0.333 inches and top edge to 0.639 inches.)

add a descriptive title

Layouts can also include static text, such as titles and section heads. We'll add a "Business Mileage" title to the title block.

1 If the Text Formatting toolbar isn't visible, choose View > Toolbars > Text Formatting.

2 Select the Text Tool (the A) and click in the dark blue title block to set the text's starting point. Choose a font and size from the Text Formatting toolbar. (I picked Verdana 24 pt., but you can use another font, such as Arial or Helvetica, for example). Set the text color to white.

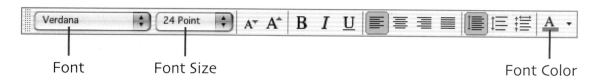

Font   Font Size   Font Color

3 Type Business Mileage. Then click outside the text block. Handles appear around the text string, and the Selection Tool (pointer) appears.

4 Click in the center of the text and drag until it's centered. (You can adjust the position by repeatedly pressing ← or →.)

place fields and labels

Now that the background graphics are in place, we can move the fields and labels into their final positions.

1 Because the background graphics were created after the fields and labels, they're in a higher layer (closer to the front). To prevent the graphics from covering the fields and labels, it's necessary to move the graphics to a lower layer. Select the graphics by ⒮Shift⒭-clicking them or by drawing a selection rectangle around them, and then choose Arrange > Send to Back.

2 Scroll to the right so you can see the fields. Because we'll want to move and place them individually, you'll have to ungroup them. Click the block of fields with the Selection Tool and choose Arrange > Ungroup.

3 Setting the color of the field and label text to black will make them easier to read against the background. And to make the field labels take up less room on the layout, we can remove the boldface.

Select only the field labels by ⒮Shift⒭-clicking or drawing a selection rectangle around them. Click the Bold icon on the Text Formatting toolbar to remove the boldface. Now draw a selection rectangle around all the fields and labels. Select black as the font color. (Windows users only: Set the font size for all fields and labels to Verdana 9 pt. rather than 10.)

4 Select both the Date field and its label as a pair by ⒮Shift⒭-clicking them. Then drag them into the upper data entry block.

5 Select the next four fields and field labels as a group (Start Mileage, End Mileage, Total Mileage, and Mileage Amount). Drag them onto the left side of the larger data entry block.

6 Select the last two fields and their labels. Drag them to the top-right side of the larger data entry block. The top of the Destination field should be aligned with the top of the Start Mileage field. (On the Size palette, check the distance of each field from the top of the layout.)

7 The distance between the labels and their fields is causing layout problems. (Text may be overlapping or spilling off the edge of the layout.) Select all the field labels and press ⒭→⒭ five times to nudge them closer to the fields.

place fields and labels

This is how the layout should look. If necessary, you can drag the field groups up or down to center them within a block. Use the Size palette to ensure that the columns of labels and fields are all aligned.

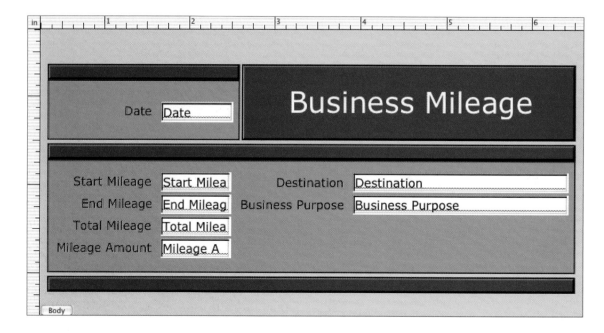

creating the data entry layout

add section labels

As you saw in the title block, you can add text on top of graphics. In fact, you can create as many layers of objects as necessary to achieve a desired effect. We'll now add white section labels on the two top graphic bars.

1 With no object selected, set the font to Verdana 9 pt. white. Select the Text Tool, click in the top bar, type Travel Date, and then click in the background. With the text block selected, use the arrow keys to vertically center the text within the bar and move it a few pixels in from the bar's left edge.

2 With the text block still selected, choose Edit > Duplicate, and then drag the copy to the same position in the second graphic bar. (Use the Size palette to ensure that the left edges of both text strings are the same distance from the left side of the window.)

3 Double-click the new text block. (Doing so selects the Text Tool.) Drag to select the text string and type Mileage.

4 The result should look like this. ———

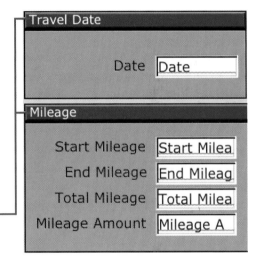

align and format fields

To ensure that the data in each field is displayed in a consistent manner from record to record, you can specify an alignment and field format settings.

1 The fields on the left side of the layout should be right-aligned, making the last digit of each of these numeric fields line up with the same digit in the other fields. Select the Date, Start Mileage, End Mileage, Total Mileage, and Mileage Amount fields, and click the Align Right icon on the Text Formatting toolbar.

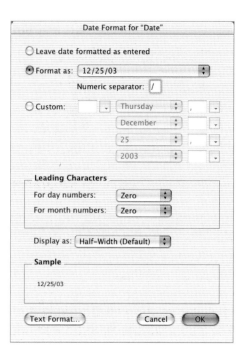

2 To set the display formatting for a field, you choose the field's data type (such as Date or Number) from the Format menu. To format the Date field, select it on the layout and choose Format > Date. Then set the following formatting options and click OK.

Format as: 12/25/03 (mm/dd/yy)
Numeric separator: / (slash)
Leading characters: Zero (for both the day and month numbers)

Dates will be displayed in the form 10/25/05. As you can see from this example, the manner in which data is displayed can be very different from how it's entered. The display depends on the formatting you've set for the field.

3 Select the first three Number fields: Start Mileage, End Mileage, and Total Mileage. Since they'll share the same formatting, we can save time by applying it to all fields at once. Choose Format > Number, set these options, and click OK.

Format as decimal: Fixed number of decimal digits (0)
Use thousands separator: , (comma)

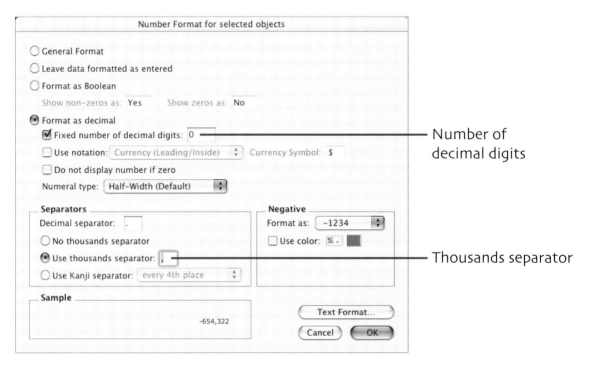

4 Mileage Amount will contain the dollars and cents value of each trip. Select the Mileage Amount field on the layout, choose Format > Number, set these options, and click OK.

Format as decimal: Fixed number of decimal digits (2)
Use notation: Currency (Leading/Inside); Currency symbol: $
Use thousands separator: , (comma)

creating the data entry layout   **43**

set the tab order

When you enter data in a layout, you press Tab to move from field to field. By default, FileMaker sets the tab order for a layout as a left-to-right, top-to-bottom sequence. Since we'll want to move through the Data Entry fields in a different order, we can create a custom tab sequence.

1 Choose Layouts > Set Tab Order. The Set Tab Order dialog box appears and a numbered arrow is displayed beside each field in the layout.

2 Change the numbers as follows: 1. Date, 2. Start Mileage, 3. End Mileage, 4. Destination, 5. Business Purpose. The numbers for Total Mileage and Mileage Amount are irrelevant because they're both Calculated fields. (You can't tab into a Calculated field.)

Edit the numbers in the tabs to match the ones shown here.

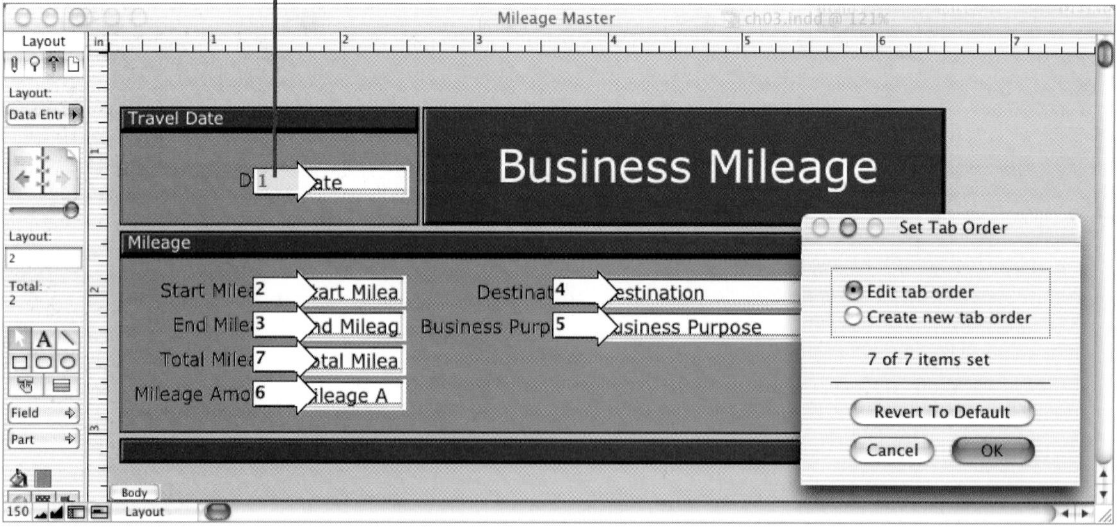

3 Click OK to set the new sequence.

save layout changes

There are some additional touches (such as scripts, buttons, and value lists) that we'll add to this layout in later chapters, but the basic elements are now in place. To see the finished layout, switch to Browse mode by choosing View > Browse Mode (⌘B/Ctrl B).

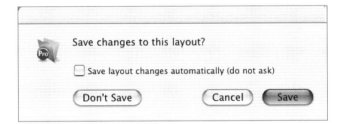

When you exit Layout mode in FileMaker Pro 7, you'll be asked if you want to save any changes you've made. Click Save. (In earlier versions of FileMaker Pro, changes are saved automatically.)

When viewed in Browse mode, this is how the Data Entry layout should look.

extra bits

use the wizard p. 26

- If you want to create a layout from scratch (instead of using one of FileMaker's colorful layout themes), choose Blank Layout in the New Layout/Report wizard.

- As you'll learn in later chapters, there will be layouts that you may not want to list in the layouts menu (found above the status area). For example, you may want to prevent users from switching directly to a report layout because it wouldn't show the proper information in Browse mode.

about layout tools p. 29

- While we'll be using the Size palette to measure distances and sizes in inches, you can also use two other measurements systems. Click the measurement unit to the right of any Size palette text box to change the units to centimeters or pixels.

remove unneeded parts p. 31

- The Part Setup dialog box is also used to add parts. Later in the book, we'll use it that way to add Subsummary parts to a report.

set field widths p. 32

- The object dimensions and locations in this chapter aren't sacred. Neither are the fonts or font sizes. The size and format of items is up to you. If you think you can improve the layout, feel free to experiment.

place fields and labels p. 39

- There are several ways to precisely align a group of fields, labels, or graphics. You can drag them to the same grid location (when object grids is enabled), set the same position on the Size palette, or choose the Arrange > Align or Set Alignment command.

- To make small adjustments to the position of a selected object, press the appropriate arrow key. This is referred to as nudging. Even with object grids enabled, you can use this technique to override the normal "snap to grid" behavior.

- If you make a mistake, immediately choose Edit > Undo. If you cannot correct a layout error this way, you can revert to the last saved version by choosing Don't Save when offered the chance to save changes.

creating the data entry layout

4. creating the global settings layout

The Global Settings layout serves two functions. First, it's where you'll enter all the constants that will be used in calculations. When we defined these fields in Chapter 2, we made them global—meaning that they were intended to store a single value for the database, rather than a different value for each record. You'll use these fields to record the IRS mileage rate for the current year (Mileage Rate), current year (Year), length of your default trip (Mileage Increment), and odometer readings at the start and end of the year (Start Mileage and End Mileage).

Second, a variety of calculations are performed on this layout. You can switch to this layout whenever you want to check the business miles driven to-date (MilesSum), as well as their dollar value (Annual Dollar). When you enter your year-end odometer reading, you'll be able to see the total miles driven for the year (Annual Miles), the split between personal and business miles (Personal Miles and MilesSum), and the dollar value of the business miles (Annual Dollar).

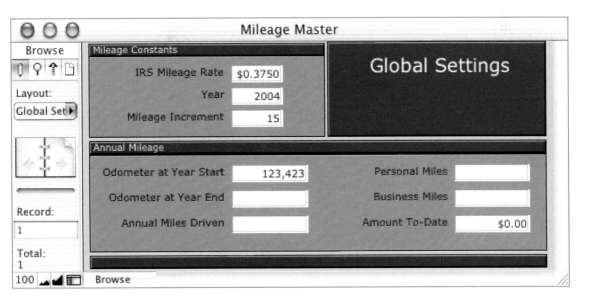

duplicate a layout

You don't have to use the New Layout/Report wizard to create every layout. Because the Global Settings layout will use many of the same design elements as the Data Entry layout, we'll create this layout by duplicating the Data Entry layout and then making the necessary changes.

1 Switch to Layout mode (View > Layout Mode).

2 Ensure that the Data Entry layout is displayed. If it isn't, choose its name from the layouts menu at the top of the status area.

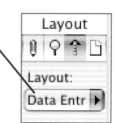

3 Choose Layouts > Duplicate Layout. A duplicate is created named Data Entry Copy and becomes the active layout.

4 To rename the layout, choose Layouts > Layout Setup.

5 Type Global Settings in the Layout Name text box, remove the check mark from Include in layouts menu, and click OK.

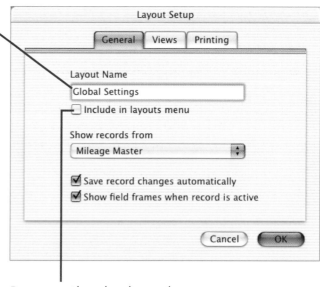

Remove the check mark

creating the global settings layout

edit the background

We'll make both of these layouts the same size. Doing so will make switching between them less visually jarring. Because the Data Entry layout will eventually contain buttons at its top (currently represented by blank space), we'll need to enlarge some of the background graphics on the Global Settings layout.

1 Switch to Layout mode and make the Global Settings layout active.

2 Select the Business Mileage text and press (Delete)/(Backspace) to delete it.

3 To enlarge the title block, select it, hold down (Shift), and drag one of the top handles upward until you reach the top of the layout. To change the block's width, select one of the handles on its left side, hold down (Shift), and drag to the right (width: 2.972 inches).

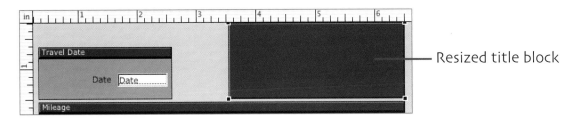

Resized title block

4 Now select both the Travel Date text and its blue bar by holding down (Shift) as you click them, and then drag them to the top of the screen. When they're in position, click a blank area of the background to deselect the two items.

5 Select only the bar (without its text). To widen it, (Shift)-drag a right handle. Stop dragging just before it reaches the title block (width = 3.181 inches).

Resized bar

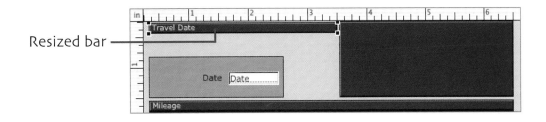

edit the background (cont.)

6 We'll resize the purple block next. Select the block and drag its upper-right handle until it's the size shown here. (Note that the block's top edge meets the bottom edge of the bar.)

Resized block   Drag this handle to resize

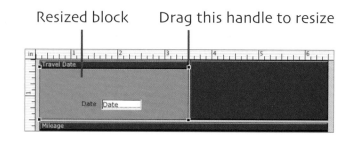

7 Now we can edit the text in the two bars. Double-click the text in the top bar. (Doing so switches to the Text Tool.) Drag-select the text and type: Mileage Constants.Then insert the word Annual in front of the Mileage text in the middle bar.

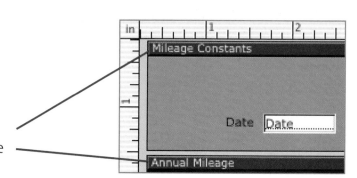

8 The layout stills needs a title. Choose a font from the Text Formatting toolbar (such as Verdana 18 pt. white), select the Text Tool, click in the title block to set the insertion point, and type Global Settings.

When you're done, click outside the title text. The text is surrounded by handles. Drag the text to approximately this position in the title block.

creating the global settings layout

replace the fields

Although we won't be using any of the duplicated fields, it's simple to substitute the correct fields for ones already on the layout.

1 While any field can be replaced with another using the procedure that follows, field labels can't be replaced. (Shift)-click all field labels on the layout and then press (Delete)/(Backspace) to delete them.

2 Double-click the Date field. In the Specify Field dialog box, select the Mileage Rate field, click the Create field label check box, and click OK.

The Mileage Rate field replaces the Date field on the layout. The formatting originally applied to the Date field is retained.

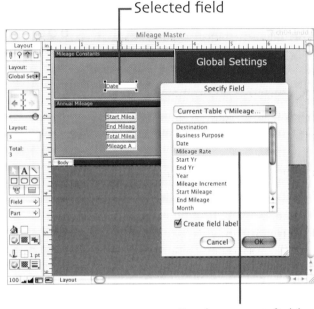

Selected field

Replacement field

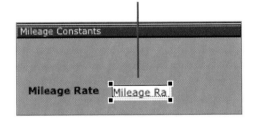

3 Using the same technique, replace Start Mileage with Year, End Mileage with Mileage Increment, Total Mileage with Start Yr, Mileage Amount with End Yr, Destination with Annual Miles, and Business Purpose with Personal Miles. Be sure to click the Create field label check box for each one.

4 Two more fields need to be added to the layout: MilesSum and Annual Dollar. To match the formatting of the other fields on the layout, the simplest way is to duplicate existing fields. Select the Personal Miles field on the layout, and choose Edit > Duplicate. In the Specify Field dialog box, select the MilesSum field, ensure that Create field label is checked, and click OK. On the layout, select the MilesSum field and its label, and drag them beneath the Personal Miles field.

replace the fields (cont.)

5 Repeat Step 4 to duplicate a field (any field in the second column will do), but this time select Annual Dollar in the Specify Field dialog box. Drag the Annual Dollar field and its field label beneath the MilesSum field.

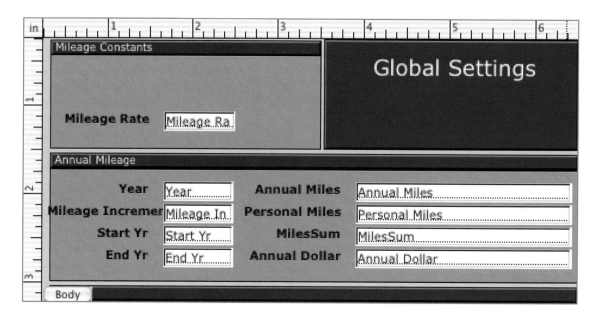

The layout should now look something like this. Don't worry about the exact placement and spacing of fields. We'll rearrange them shortly.

creating the global settings layout

set formatting

To complete the layout, we need to reformat the labels; edit the label text; set the size, alignment, and formatting for the fields; and move the label/field pairs to the proper spots. The table below shows many of the important format settings for the fields and labels.

1 Select all field labels and set these options on the Text Formatting toolbar: Verdana, 10 pt. (Mac), 9 pt. (PC), not bold, black, right-aligned. (We want to duplicate the label formatting from the Data Entry layout. If you chose a different font or size for that layout, use the same formatting here, too.)

2 One by one, select the Mileage Rate, Year, and Mileage Increment field. Set each one's width to 0.681 inches. Then select each remaining field on the layout, and set its width to 1.014 inches.

Field Name	Field Label	Number Formatting Options
Mileage Rate	IRS Mileage Rate	Format as decimal, 4 decimal digits; Use notation: Currency (leading/inside), $ symbol; no thousands separator
Year	Year	Format as decimal, 0 decimal digits; no thousands separator
Mileage Increment	Mileage Increment	Format as decimal, 0 decimal digits; no thousands separator
Start Yr	Odometer at Year Start	Format as decimal, 0 decimal digits; thousands separator: , (comma)
End Yr	Odometer at Year End	Format as decimal, 0 decimal digits; thousands separator: , (comma)
Annual Miles	Annual Miles Driven	Format as decimal, 0 decimal digits; thousands separator: , (comma)
Personal Miles	Personal Miles	Format as decimal, 0 decimal digits; thousands separator: , (comma)
MilesSum	Business Miles	Format as decimal, 0 decimal digits; thousands separator: , (comma)
Annual Dollar	Amount To-Date	Format as decimal, 2 decimal digits; Use notation: Currency (leading/inside), $ symbol; thousands separator: , (comma)

creating the global settings layout 53

set formatting (cont.)

3 Select all fields and set their paragraph alignment to right-aligned.

4 All fields on this layout will store numbers. Select each field, choose Format > Number, and set the number formatting options listed in the table.

5 Using the Text Tool, edit the field labels as indicated in the table.

Sanity check: Your layout should now look similar to this. Because of their length, some labels automatically shifted right in order to remain on the layout. Don't worry; we'll fix them in the next section.

arrange the fields

Now it's time to move the fields and their labels into the proper positions.

1 Select the four fields and matching labels on the right side of the layout, and [Shift]-drag them to the right edge. (They won't remain there, but we'll need to get them out of the way to give us room to work.)

2 Select the same four field's labels (as shown here) by [Shift]-clicking them. Press [→] five times to move the labels closer to their fields.

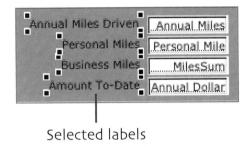

Selected labels

3 [Shift]-drag the five fields on the left side of the layout slightly to the right, away from their field labels.

4 After you edited the five field's labels, their right edges were no longer aligned with one another. Select these five field labels and choose Arrange > Set Alignment. In the Set Alignment dialog box, choose None and Align right edges. Then click OK.

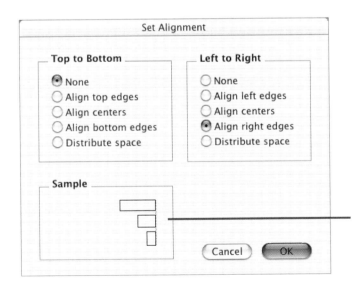

Check the Sample box to determine how the selected items will be aligned with one another.

arrange the fields (cont.)

5 The Mileage Constants block (top left) will hold three fields: Mileage Rate, Year, and Mileage Increment. Arrange these fields and labels in a single column. Move the labels so they're closer to their fields, as was done for the previous fields.

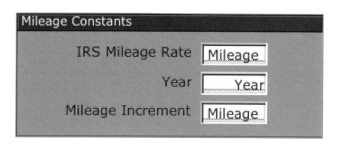

If you increase the zoom level, you'll find it easier to create the same spacing between fields, as well as center them vertically within the block. Use the arrow keys to nudge them into position, if necessary.

6 The remaining fields should be arranged in the Annual Mileage block as shown below. (In both columns of three, the right edges of the labels are aligned and the top of each field is aligned with the top of the field in the other column. Use the Size palette to check positions.)

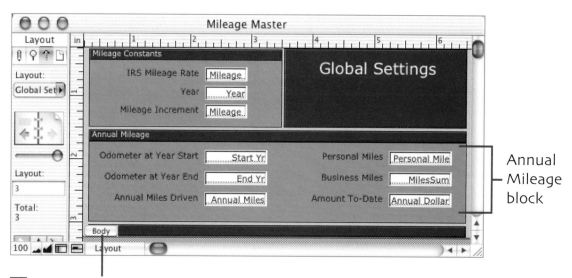

7 At present, there's space between the Body tab and the bottom bar. Eliminate the space by dragging the Body tab up to the bottom edge of the lower bar (as shown above).

creating the global settings layout

8 To finalize the layout, choose View > Browse Mode. When prompted to save your changes, click Save. (This dialog box is a new feature in FileMaker Pro 7. If you have an earlier version, the Save changes dialog box won't appear. Instead, all layout changes are saved automatically.)

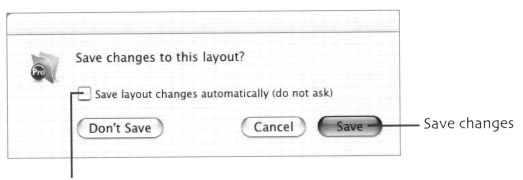

Save changes

Click to automatically save all future layout changes (without presenting this dialog box)

As is the case with the Data Entry layout, the Global Settings layout isn't completely finished. In Chapter 8, we'll add a button that—when clicked—takes you to the Data Entry layout.

extra bits

replace the fields p. 51

- Another way to add a field is to click the Insert Field tool and drag the new field onto the layout.

- When moving a field and its label, you may want to group the two items to avoid accidentally losing the original alignment and spacing between them. Select the field and label, and choose Arrange > Group.

set formatting p. 53

- On a PC, FileMaker Pro initially lists only a handful of fonts in the Format > Font submenu. To add other fonts, choose Format > Font > Configure/More Fonts.

- You can open the Number Format dialog box by [Ctrl]/right-clicking a Number field and choosing Number Format from the menu that pops up.

- When applying formatting to Number fields, you can speed up the process by applying it to several fields at once. For example, Year and Mileage Increment share the same Number formatting, so it can be applied to both of them simultaneously.

- You can also resize several fields simultaneously by typing values into the Size palette. However, they must initially all be the same size.

arrange the fields p. 55

- After using the Set Alignment dialog box, you can apply the same alignment settings to a new group of selected items by choosing Arrange > Align. Until you specify new settings in the Set Alignment dialog box, the current ones are remembered.

- You can also use the Set Alignment dialog box to distribute a group of items (spacing them equidistant from one another). For example, on this layout, group each field and label pair in a column. Move the uppermost and the lowermost fields to their intended spots on the layout. Then select all fields in the column and choose Arrange > Set Alignment. Select Distribute Space in the Top to Bottom section and None in the Left to Right section.

creating the global settings layout

5. creating the blank forms layout

Unless you intend to rush home to record your mileage after every business-related trip, you'll need another way to keep track of trips in your vehicle. Most people simply carry a trip log in the vehicle and record each trip as it occurs.

Although you can buy a trip log at most stationery and business supply stores, it's just as simple to create one in FileMaker Pro. In this chapter, you'll create the Blank Forms layout. Later in the book, we'll create a script that will automatically print a year's supply of log forms.

The Blank Forms layout includes four copies of the form per page.

create the layout

Normally, a form like this would be created using FileMaker's drawing tools (the Line Tool and Rectangle Tool). In fact, that's the way I did create it. While you're welcome to re-create it using the same method, it's considerably more work than most people are prepared to do. To help you put this form together with minimal effort, a graphic version of the form background (blankform.tif) is included in the Web site download (www.siliconwasteland.com/fmp.htm).

In case you want to take a stab at it, here's the original version of the form as it looks in Layout mode with all objects selected.

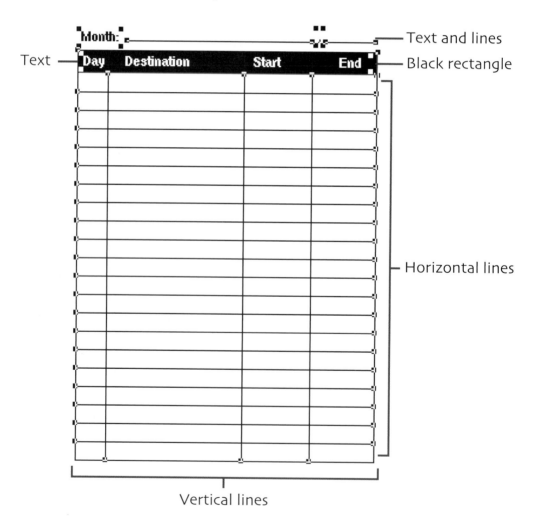

The version of the form that we're about to create only requires that we place the text strings onto the background graphic. Adding the text within FileMaker rather than providing it as part of the graphic ensures that laser printers will treat it as real text instead of just a mass of dots. Thus, it will be clear and crisp.

1 Switch to Layout mode (View > Layout Mode).

2 Choose Layouts > New Layout/Report.

3 In the New Layout/Report wizard, enter Blank Forms as the Layout Name. Remove the check mark from Include in layouts menu, select the Blank layout from the layout type list, and click Finish. The blank layout appears.

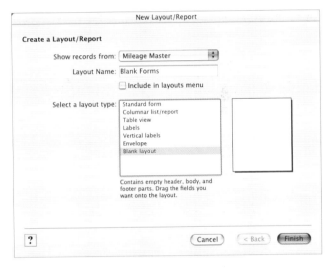

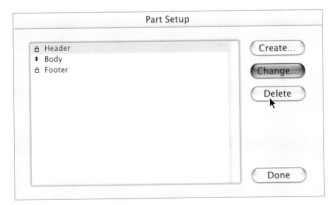

4 Like the layouts we've already created, this one needs only a Body part—not a Header or Footer. Choose Layouts > Part Setup. In the Part Setup dialog box, select and delete the Header part. Then do the same for the Footer part. Click Done to dismiss the dialog box.

create the layout (cont.)

5 The layout will fill and be printed on an 8 ½" x 11" page. Choose File > Page Setup/Print Setup. Ensure that your destination printer and portrait mode are selected. Choosing the correct printer sets the default margins for the printout.

6 Increase the height of the document window by dragging the bottom-right corner. Then drag the Body tab downward until it is just above the bottom page break indicator—somewhere between the 10 ³⁄₈" and 10 ⁷⁄₈" marks on the vertical graphic ruler. (If the rulers aren't visible, choose View > Graphic Rulers.)

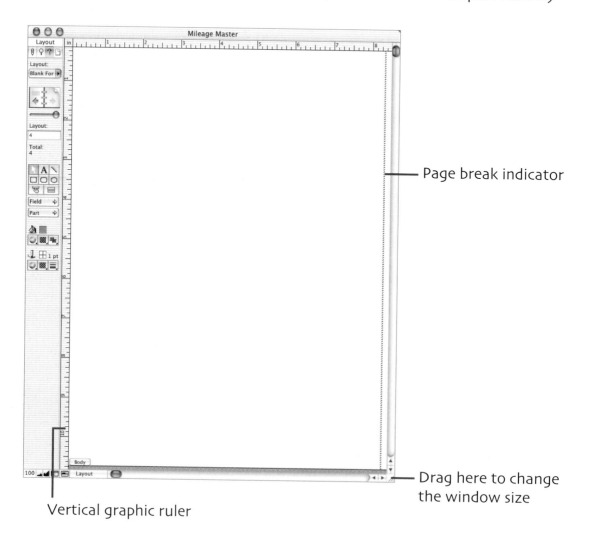

Page break indicator

Vertical graphic ruler

Drag here to change the window size

creating the blank forms layout

7 If you haven't already done so, download the Mac or Windows graphic archive from my Web site: www.siliconwasteland.com/fmp.htm. Extract the contents of the archive to a convenient location, such as the Desktop.

If you are a Macintosh user, you'll need the free StuffIt Extractor or StuffIt Deluxe (www.allume.com) to open the archive. Windows users can use WinZip; a free trial version is available at www.winzip.com/downwzeval.htm.

8 To place the image on the layout, choose Insert > Picture. In the Insert Picture dialog box, navigate to the folder in which the graphics are stored, select the blankform.tif file, ensure that Store only a reference to the file is not checked, and click Open.

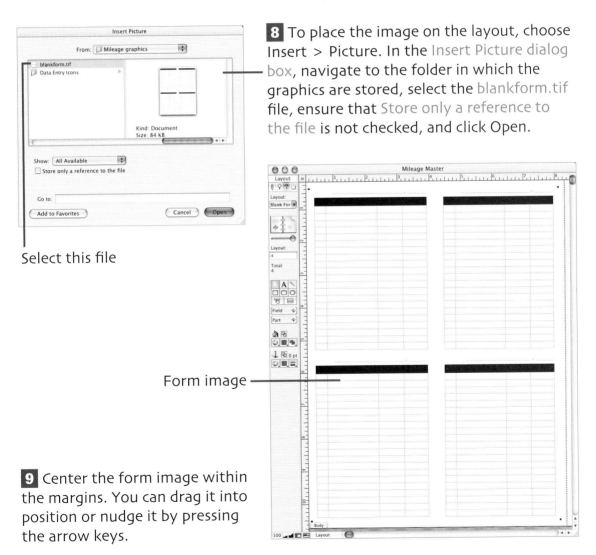

Select this file

Form image

9 Center the form image within the margins. You can drag it into position or nudge it by pressing the arrow keys.

add the text

All that's left is to add the text strings to the top of the four copies of the log form.

1 Select the Text Tool. Set the insertion point to the left of the line at the top of the first log form and choose font settings from the Text Formatting toolbar (for example, Arial 12 pt., bold, black, left-aligned).

2 Type Month: and click in a blank area at the edge of the layout. Doing so will cause the Month text string to be selected.

3 Choose View > T-Squares. The T-Squares are a pair of lines—horizontal and vertical—that you can drag to new locations and use to help place objects. Drag the vertical line so it runs along the left side of the dark block on the first form. Drag the horizontal line to where it matches the underline above the dark block. Finally, use the arrow keys to nudge the Month text block so its left and bottom edges align with the intersection of the T-Squares.

T-Squares vertical line

Align the Month text with the T-Squares lines.

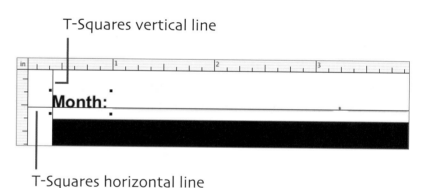

T-Squares horizontal line

4 Select the Text Tool again and set the insertion point inside the black block near its left end. Choose settings for the column heading text from the Text Formatting toolbar (for example, Arial 10 pt., bold, white, left-aligned). The text must be a light color in order for it to be readable within the black block.

5 Type Day Destination Start End. Click in a blank area at the edge of the layout, causing the text to be selected. Nudge the text so that Day is just inside of and vertically centered within the black box. Insert spaces or tabs into the text string to position each heading over its column (as shown on the next page).

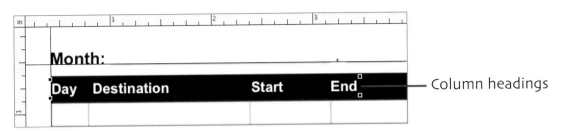

Column headings

6 Using the Selection Tool, [Shift]-click the two text strings (Month: and Day Destination Start End) to select them, and then choose Edit > Duplicate. Copies of the two text strings appear. With the copies selected, drag them into position on the blank form to the right. Use the Size palette to ensure that the copies and the originals are the same distance from the top of the layout.

7 Using the Selection Tool, [Shift]-click all four text strings to select them, and then choose Edit > Duplicate. Position the copies directly over the originals by pressing [←] and [↑] six times apiece. (Zoom in to check their positions.) With all four items selected, [Shift]-drag them down into position on the remaining pair of blank forms.

8 When you're satisfied with the text string's positions, choose Edit > Select All to select all items on the layout. Then choose Arrange > Group to treat the graphic and text as a single entity.

9 Choose View > Preview Mode so you can see how the page will look when it's printed (see page 59). When prompted to save your changes, click Save.

extra bits

create the layout p. 60

- While this layout could be included in the layouts menu, it's a better practice to only include layouts that the user needs to be able to switch to manually. The Blank Forms layout never needs to be viewed; it's for printing only.

- The graphic must fit entirely within the Body part, and the Body must not extend beyond one page. If it's longer than a page (indicated by a page break indicator at the bottom), each copy of the form will print two pages: one with the form and one blank.

- While creating this form, feel free to reset the zoom (magnification). Zoom out to center the image and zoom in to place the text.

add the text p. 64

- When moving [Shift]-clicked items, it's easy to accidentally deselect one of the items when conducting the move. If you notice this happening, click the deselected item again and then make the move.

- You can also duplicate selected items by choosing Edit > Copy followed by Edit > Paste.

- Switching to any mode (not just Preview mode) will cause the layout changes to be saved. Prior to making major changes to a layout, it's a good idea to force a save in this manner. You can also save changes at any time by choosing Layouts > Save Layout (⌘ S / Ctrl S).

- Although we only eyeballed the form graphic when placing it on the layout, the key to whether it's properly centered is in how it prints. Since everything was grouped at the end, you can easily adjust the entire form's position without being concerned that the text strings will slip and slide.

creating the blank forms layout

6. creating the monthly totals report

Now comes the fun part—and the reason you've chosen to painstakingly record your trips in a database. We're going to create reports to summarize the data. Each report can be set up in the New Layout/Report wizard (with which you're already very familiar). Like other FileMaker reports, the reports you'll create can be printed or viewed onscreen in Preview mode.

We'll create scripts in Chapter 8 so you can generate the two reports: the Mileage Report (monthly totals) and the Destination breakdown report.

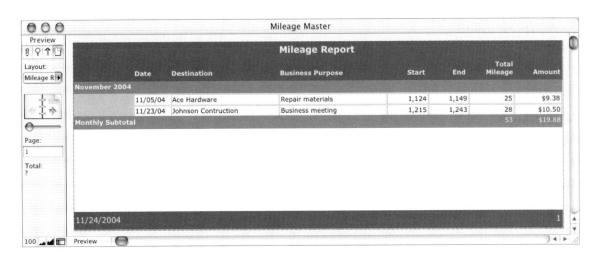

The Mileage Report produces a separate page for each month.

create the basic layout

1 Switch to Layout mode (View > Layout Mode).

2 Choose Layouts > New Layout/Report.

3 In the New Layout/Report wizard, enter Mileage Report as the name. Remove the check mark from Include in layouts menu, select the Columnar list/ report type, and click Next.

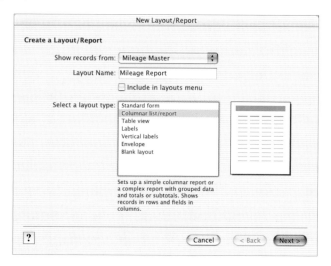

4 On the Choose Report Layout screen, select Report with grouped data, click both check boxes, and then click Next.

The report will compute monthly subtotals, as well as a grand total.

Move fields into this list

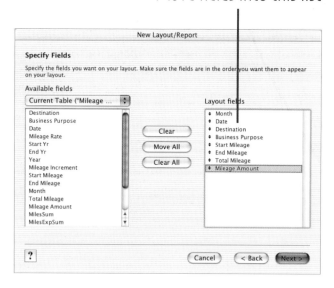

5 On the Specify Fields screen, select and move fields into the Layout fields list in the following order: Month, Date, Destination, Business Purpose, Start Mileage, End Mileage, Total Mileage, Mileage Amount. Click Next to continue.

6 On the Organize Records by Category screen, select Month as the field on which records will be grouped (summarized). Click Next to continue.

creating the monthly totals report

7 On the Sort Records screen, the Month field is already included in the Sort order list. Move the Start Mileage field into the list, and click Next.

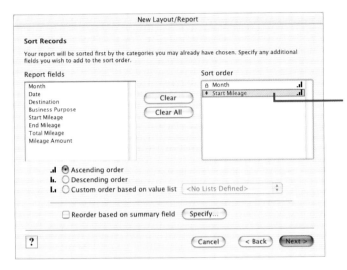

Move fields into the Sort order list in the same way that you previously selected fields to include in the layout.

8 We want monthly subtotals on two Summary fields: MilesSum (total mileage) and MilesExpSum (total mileage dollar value). On the Specify Subtotals screen, set these options: Summary field: MilesSum, summarize by Month, Below record group. Then click Add Subtotal. To create the next subtotal, set MilesExpSum as the Summary field, leave the other settings as they are, and click Add Subtotal. Click Next to continue.

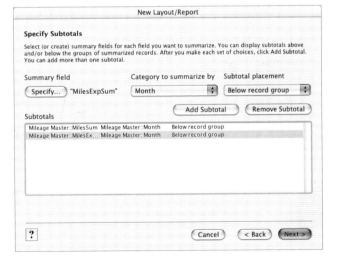

create the basic layout

9 On the Specify Grand Totals screen, we'll generate grand totals for the report using the same Summary fields: MilesSum and MilesExpSum. Set Summary field: MilesSum, End of report; and then click Add Grand Total. Then set Summary field: MilesExpSum, End of report; and click Add Grand Total. Click Next.

10 On the Select a Theme screen, we'll select the initial format for the layout. FileMaker provides two versions of most themes: one for screen and another for print (although they're occasionally identical). Select Ocean Blue Screen and click Next.

11 On the Header and Footer Information screen, we'll specify the text that will appear in the header and footer of each report page. For the header, choose Layout Name as the Top center item. For the footer, choose Current Date for the Bottom left item and Page Number for the Bottom right item. Click Next.

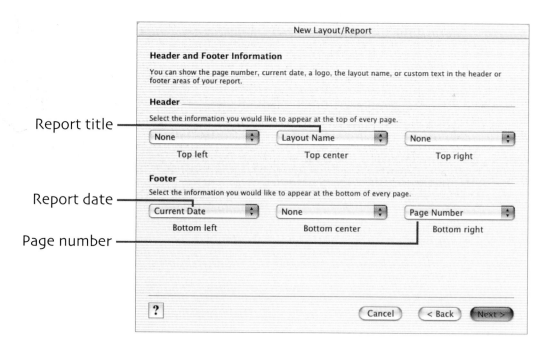

12 On the Create a Script for This Report screen, select Do not create a script and then click Next. (Although this report will be generated by running a script, we'll construct the script manually in Chapter 8.)

13 On the final screen, select View the report in Layout mode and click Finish.

Date symbol   Page number symbol

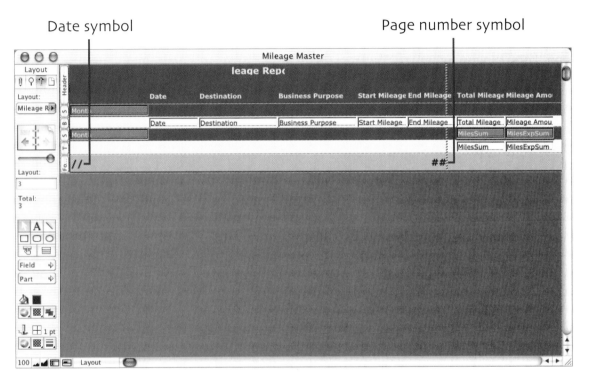

This is how the wizard-generated layout should look.

edit the layout

FileMaker's theme layouts often leave much to be desired, so I generally modify them. In this section and the ones that follow, we'll make the changes needed to turn the wizard-generated layout into an attractive report layout.

1 As you can see, the layout isn't wide enough to comfortably accommodate all the fields. To correct this, choose File > Page Setup/Print Setup, ensure that the correct destination printer is chosen, and set the orientation to Landscape. (On a PC, the option is labeled Landscape; on a Mac, click the second or third icon.)

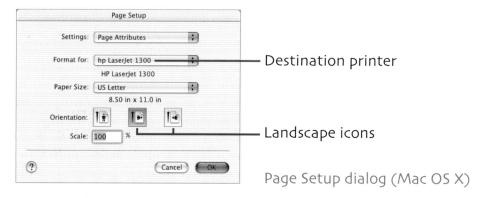

Destination printer

Landscape icons

Page Setup dialog (Mac OS X)

2 To enlarge and fully display the report title, drag one of its handles. Then center the title on the page.

3 All Number fields should be right- rather than left-aligned. On the layout, select the Start Mileage field and all fields to the right of it. Click the Align Right icon on the Text Formatting toolbar.

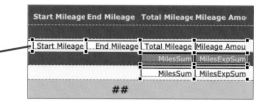

4 Format the Date field (as shown previously on page 42) by selecting it on the layout, choosing Format > Date, and setting these options: Format as 12/25/03, separator: /; Leading Characters: Zero (for both day and month numbers).

creating the monthly totals report

5 Select the Mileage Amount field and the two MilesExpSum fields. Choose Format > Number and set these options: Format as decimal, 2 decimal digits; Use notation: Currency (Leading/Inside), $; Use thousands separator: , (comma).

6 Select the remaining Number fields: Start Mileage, End Mileage, Total Mileage, and the two MilesSum fields. Choose Format > Number and set these options: Format as decimal, 0 decimal digits; Use thousands separator: , (comma).

7 For the sake of clarity, each report page should display the year as well as the month. Select the top Month field on the layout and choose Edit > Duplicate. In the Specify Field dialog box, select the Year field, remove the check mark from Create field label, and click OK. Drag the Year field to the right of the Month field.

Add the Year field beside the Month field in the Subsummary part directly below the Header.

8 Select the Month and Year fields. Choose Format > Sliding/Printing. In the Set Sliding/Printing dialog box, click the Sliding left check box and then click OK. Setting this option will cause the space between the two text strings to close up when printed or viewed in Preview mode.

9 Delete the Month field in the lower Subsummary part. Select the Text Tool and add the following text string in the same spot: Monthly Subtotal. Add a Grand Total text string in the Trailing Grand Summary part immediately below it.

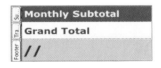

10 Align the right edge of the page number placeholder with the right edge of the MilesExpSum field, correctly positioning the placeholder for landscape mode printing.

11 Switch to Browse mode, and save the layout changes when prompted. Choose the Data Entry layout from the layouts pop-up menu in the status area.

creating the monthly totals report 73

12 Create several sample records for at least two months and enter some test data into the fields on the Global Settings layout so you can test the report layout. To create the new records, choose Records > New Record.

13 In order for the data to be grouped by month, you must sort the database before previewing or printing the report. Choose Records > Sort Records. Click Sort in the Sort Records dialog box that appears.

14 To display the report, switch to Layout mode, choose Mileage Report from the layouts menu, and then choose View > Preview Mode.

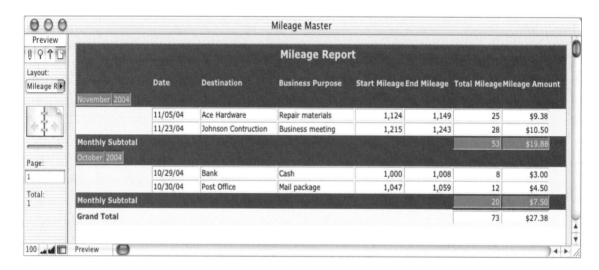

Including at least two months in the test data enables the report to be broken into separate months. However, the months are listed alphabetically. In Chapter 8, we'll define a value list that contains the months in their proper order and modify the sort to use that order.

15 You'll note that all months are on the same report page. To display one month per page, return to Layout mode, choose Layouts > Part Setup, double-click Sub-summary by Month (Trailing), click the Page break after every 1 occurrence check box, click OK, and then click Done.

change part colors

The Header and both Subsummary parts in this theme are colored with a custom color; that is, it isn't a standard color in the FileMaker Pro Mac or Windows color palette. We'll use this custom color to also color the Trailing Grand Summary and Footer parts of the layout. Separate instructions are provided below for working with custom colors on a Macintosh and a PC.

Custom Colors on a Macintosh

1 In Layout mode, display the Mileage Report. Click the Header tab.

2 Click the Fill Color icon and choose Other Color (at the bottom of the palette).

3 In the Colors dialog box that appears, the Header's custom color is shown as a color bar.

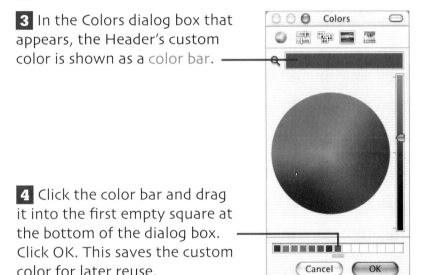

4 Click the color bar and drag it into the first empty square at the bottom of the dialog box. Click OK. This saves the custom color for later reuse.

5 Click the Trailing Grand Summary tab on the layout. (It's the section with the Grand Total text.) Click the Fill Pattern icon and select the solid fill pattern. Then choose Other Color from the bottom of the Fill Color palette. Click the custom color's square at the bottom of the Colors dialog box and then click OK.

6 Click the Footer tab, choose Other Color from the bottom of the Fill Color palette, click the custom color's square in the Colors dialog box, and click OK.

Fill Color icon
Fill Pattern icon
Solid fill

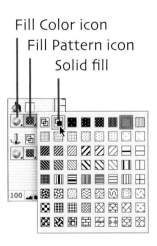

change part colors (cont.)

Custom Colors on a Windows PC

1 In Layout mode, display the Mileage Report. Click the Header tab.

2 Click the Fill Color icon and choose Other Color (at the bottom of the palette).

3 To save the Header's custom color, click Add to Custom Colors. Click OK.

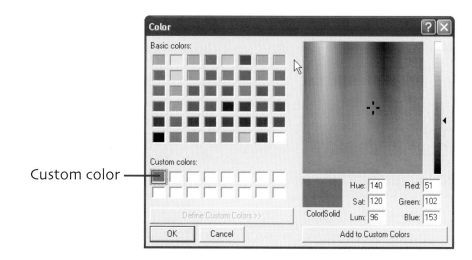

Custom color

4 Click the Trailing Grand Summary tab on the layout. (It's the section with the Grand Total text.) Click the Fill Pattern icon and select the solid fill pattern (as shown on the previous page). Then click the Fill Color palette and choose Other Color. In the Color dialog box, click the custom color's square and then click OK.

5 To apply the custom color to the Footer, click the Footer tab, choose Other Color from the bottom of the Fill Color palette, click the custom color's square in the Color dialog box, and then click OK.

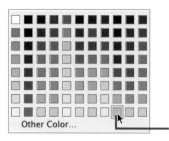

Click this color

Change the Body color. The blue used for the Body is too light for my taste. Click the Body tab. Click the Fill Color icon and select the shade of blue shown here.

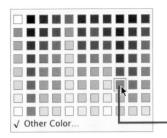

√ Other Color...

Set the Subsummary color. To color these two parts (the upper one contains the Month and Year fields; the lower contains the Monthly Subtotal text), click each one's tab and select this color. Also select the two fields in each of these parts and apply the same color to them.

———— Click this color

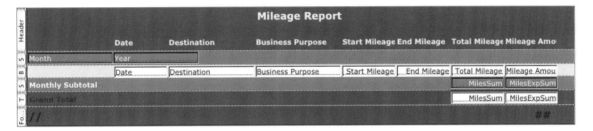

Here's what the layout should look like now.

format text and fields

Format the section titles. To make the title text in the two Subsummary parts the same, select the Month and Year fields on the layout, and click the Bold icon on the Text Formatting toolbar.

Remove 3-D formatting. Select the fields in both Subsummary parts (Month, Year, MilesSum, MilesExpSum) and in the Trailing Grand Summary part (MilesSum, MilesExpSum). Set the Effect to None to remove the 3-D formatting that was originally applied to these fields.

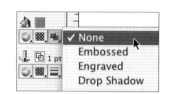

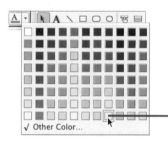

Format the Trailing Grand Summary and Footer text. The text in these two parts should be the same color as the other label text. Select the Grand Total text string, the MilesSum and MilesExpSum fields, and the pair of symbols in the Footer. On the Text Formatting toolbar, select this text color.

Set field color in the Trailing Grand Summary. The MilesSum and MilesExpSum fields in the Trailing Grand Summary should be the same custom color as the part. Select both fields, choose Other Color from the bottom of the Fill Color palette, and select the custom color that you previously applied to this layout part.

Remove the field borders. Because the fields in the Subsummary (Trailing) and the Trailing Grand Summary are already in a contrasting type color, there's no need for them to have borders, too. To remove the borders, select the two MilesSum fields and the two MilesExpSum fields, and choose Format > Field Borders. In the Field Borders dialog box, clear all check marks and then click OK.

To clear borders from selected fields, remove all check marks.

Format the Footer text. Select both symbols in the Footer. Using the Text Formatting toolbar, reduce the font size to 12 pt. and remove the boldface.

Delete the lines. There are two lines beneath the MilesSum and MilesExpSum fields in the Subsummary by Month (Trailing) part. Select them and press ⌷Delete⌷/⌷Backspace⌷.

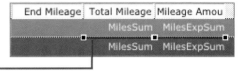

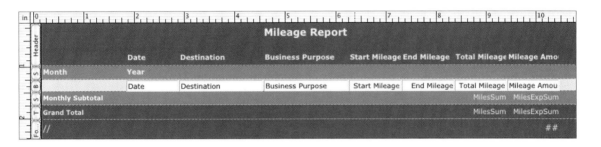

This is how the layout should look now.

Edit the field labels. Four of the field labels in the Header are too long to fit comfortably on the layout. Using the Text Tool, change Start Mileage to Start, End Mileage to End, and Mileage Amount to Amount. Reduce the width of the Total Mileage label until it splits into two lines. Align its bottom edge with that of the other field labels. Eliminate some of the excess width for these labels and right-align their text. Align the right edges of the four labels with the right edges of the corresponding data fields below.

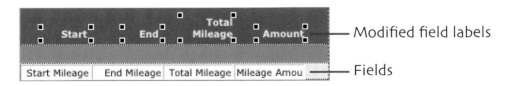

— Modified field labels

— Fields

make final adjustments

All that's left to finish the layout is to resize the fields to match the data they'll contain and then move everything into their final positions.

1 Using the Size palette, set the following field widths (in inches) in the Body: Date: 0.792, Destination and Business Purpose: 2.333, Start Mileage and End Mileage: 0.875, Total Mileage: 0.986, Mileage Amount: 1.042.

2 Select each of the following labels and then use the Size palette to set its distance from the left edge as follows: Date: 1.486, Destination: 2.292, Business Purpose: 4.639. For each matching field, set the same distance from the left edge.

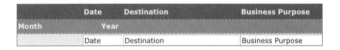

Here are the Date, Destination, and Business Purpose labels and fields in their new positions.

3 The remaining Body fields and labels are all right-aligned. Select each label, and use the Size palette to set the distance from its right edge as follows: Start Mileage: 7.861, End Mileage: 8.750, Total Mileage: 9.750, Mileage Amount: 10.806. Then select the corresponding field and set the same distance from its right edge.

4 Set the right-edge distance of the two MilesSum fields to 9.750 and the right-edge distance of the two MilesExpSum fields to 10.806.

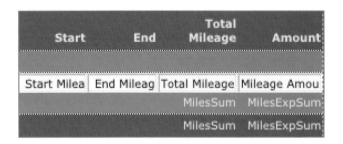

These numeric Body fields are right-aligned. Here's how they'll look after being moved to their final positions on the layout.

5 Select the Monthly Subtotal text string and use the Size palette to determine the distance from its left edge. Ensure that Month, Grand Total, and the Date placeholder (//) are all the same distance from their left edges.

6 Select the Page Number placeholder (# #) and set its right edge distance to 10.806 inches. Doing so aligns its right edge with the right edge of the layout elements directly above it.

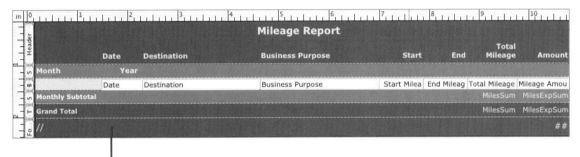

This is the finished layout (above). To view the report it generates (below), switch to Preview mode. Click the Book pages to see any additional report pages.

Book

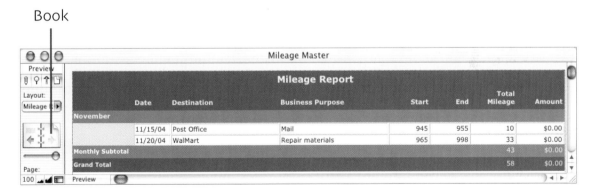

extra bits

create the basic layout p. 68

- You'll note in Step 5 that Month was included in the field list. Although you aren't required to place it in the final layout, you must include it in the field list in order to use it as the grouping field in Step 6.

- Subtotals and grand totals must be based on Summary fields. This is because only Summary fields are designed to perform calculations across multiple records.

- The initial position of the page break in the generated layout is determined by the Page Setup or Print Setup setting (portrait or landscape) in effect at the time.

edit the layout p. 72

- As you make the layout changes, it's a good idea to periodically switch to Preview mode to see their effect. Be sure to save your layout changes when prompted.

- In FileMaker Pro 7, you can also save layout changes by pressing ⌘Ⓢ or choosing Layouts > Save Layout.

- Don't worry about the accuracy of your sample data. We'll delete all records before entering the real data.

change part colors p. 75

- You can also use the Colors/Color dialog box to create your own custom colors. Select the object to be colored, choose Other Color from the Fill Color palette, and use the dialog box controls to select and add the new color.

format text and fields p. 78

- You can apply the 3-D Emboss effect to field labels for an attractive look.

- Another way to copy formatting from a selected object to another object is to use the Format Painter tool. Select the first object, click the Format Painter icon on the Standard toolbar, and then click the destination object.

- When resizing and rearranging fields or labels, it's easy for them to slip out of alignment. You can use the Arrange > Set Alignment command to align these objects along their bottom edges. Note, however, that all selected objects will be aligned to the lowest of the objects.

7. creating the destination report

When you need another report from a database, it isn't always necessary to create the report from scratch. Many are simply variations of existing reports. We've already created a Mileage Report that groups trips by month (refer to Chapter 6). To create a new report that is similar to the first one, we can duplicate the initial report and then make any necessary changes to the fields, Subsummary parts, and sort instructions. In this chapter, we'll duplicate the Mileage Report and modify the duplicate to create a destination-based report, enabling you to quickly see your year-to-date mileage for each destination, as well as the number of trips to each destination.

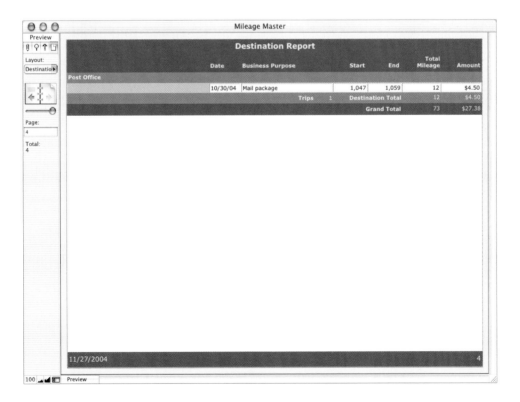

duplicate the layout

1 Switch to Layout mode (View > Layout Mode).

2 Ensure that the Mileage Report layout is displayed. If it isn't, choose its name from the layouts menu at the top of the status area.

3 Choose Layouts > Duplicate Layout. A duplicate is created named Mileage Report Copy and becomes the active layout.

4 To rename the layout, choose Layouts > Layout Setup. The Layout Setup dialog box appears.

5 Enter Destination Report in the Layout Name text box, remove the check mark from Include in layouts menu, and then click OK to dismiss the dialog box.

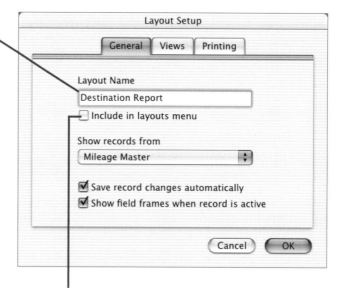

Remove the check mark

creating the destination report

group by destination

The sort field associated with a Subsummary is responsible for breaking the data into groups. In the Mileage Report, Month is the field on which the leading Sub-summary is sorted, resulting in a separate group for each month. Because the Destination Report will be grouped by destination, we need to change the leading Subsummary's part definition to use Destination as the sort field.

1 In Layout mode with the Destination Report layout selected, choose Layouts > Part Setup.

2 In the Part Setup dialog box, select Sub-summary by Month (Leading) and click Change.

3 In the Part Definition dialog box, select Sub-summary when sorted by, select Destination in the field list, ensure that no check boxes are checked, and click OK. Click Done to dismiss the Part Setup dialog box.

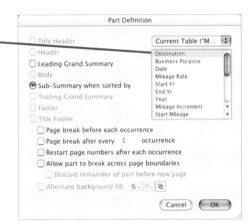

4 On the layout, delete the Year field from the Subsummary part by selecting the field and pressing [Delete]/[Backspace].

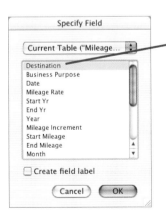

5 Double-click the Month field to replace it. In the Specify Field dialog box, select the Destination field, ensure that Create field label is unchecked, and click OK. Month is replaced on the layout by Destination.

6 Widen the Destination field to 2.5" by selecting the field and [Shift]-dragging one of the handles on its right side.

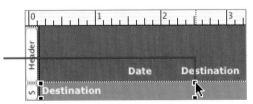

refine the layout

Delete the Destination field and label. Since the destination is now listed in the leading Subsummary, there's no point in repeating it within the Body part. We'll need to delete the field and close up the gap that the deletion leaves.

1 Select the Destination field in the Body part and press Delete/Backspace.

2 Select the Destination label in the Header and press Delete/Backspace.

3 Shift-click the Date field (in the body) and the Date label (in the Header) to select them as a pair. Drag the pair to the right to close up the gap made by the deletion of the Destination field.

Correct the title. Using the Text Tool, edit the title to read Destination Report. Drag the title to center it on the 5.5" mark on the horizontal graphic ruler.

Here are the changes you've made so far.

Destination field in the leading Subsummary

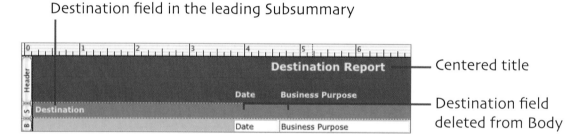

Centered title

Destination field deleted from Body

Change the title in the trailing Subsummary. Using the Text Tool, edit the Monthly Subtotal text in the trailing Subsummary to read Destination Total. Click the Align Right icon on the Text Formatting toolbar.

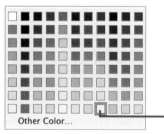

Set the color of the Destination Total text to match the color of the Miles Sum and MilesExpSum fields to the right of it.

Select this color from the Text Formatting toolbar.

Align the Destination Total text. Use the Size palette to set the Destination Total text's position at 8.750 inches from its right edge (aligning it with the right edge of the End Mileage field directly above it).

Modify the Grand Total text. Using the Selection Tool, select the Grand Total text in the Trailing Grand Summary. Click the Align Right icon on the Text Formatting toolbar. Use the Size palette to set the Destination Total text's position at 8.750 inches from its right edge, aligning it with the Destination Total text.

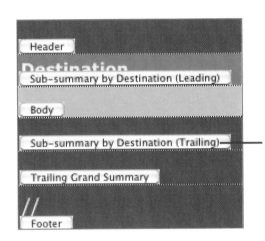

Color the trailing Subsummary. Click the trailing Subsummary tab and make it the same custom color as the Header, Trailing Grand Summary, and Footer.

Select this tab and assign it the same custom color.

Transparent text backgrounds. To make a text string or field blend with the background color, you can either set the string or field's fill color to the background color or set its pattern to transparent.

Select the three items in the trailing Subsummary (the Destination Total text and the two fields) and set their fill pattern to transparent.

Transparent

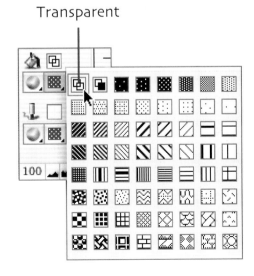

creating the destination report

create a trip count field

To make the summary statistics a little more useful, we'll create a new Summary field that will display the trip count (number of trips) for each destination.

1 Switch to Layout mode and ensure that the Destination Report layout is displayed. Choose File > Define > Database.

2 Switch to the Fields tab of the Define Database dialog box. Enter Trips as the Field Name for the new field, choose Summary from the Type pop-up menu, and click Create.

Field Name   Field Type

3 On the Options for Summary Field "Trips" dialog box, select Count of as the summary statistic and select Destination in the Available Fields list as the field to summarize. Click OK and then OK again to dismiss the dialog boxes. The new field and its label are placed in the Body part.

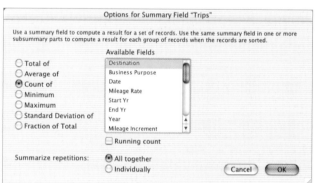

4 Shift-select the Trips label and field. Drag them into position in the trailing Subsummary (as shown below). To remove the extra space at the bottom of the Body part, drag the bottom of the Body part up as high as it will go.

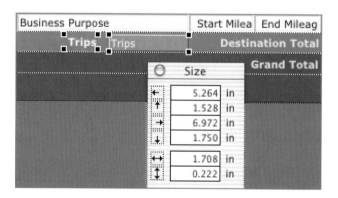

5 For the label and field, set a distance from the right edge of 6.972 inches and distance from top of 1.528 inches. (Align the field's right edge with the right edge of the Business Purpose field. Align the top of the Trips label and field with the top of the Destination Total label.)

6 Now we need to format the Trips field and label. Select the Destination Total text string, click the Format Painter icon on the Standard toolbar, and click the Trips label. Now select the MilesSum field (beside the Destination Total text string), click the Format Painter icon on the Standard toolbar, and click the Trips field.

7 Reduce the width of the Trips field by dragging one of its left-hand handles to the right. (The field only needs to be wide enough to show three digits.) Finally, Shift-drag the Trips label to the right to close up the gap.

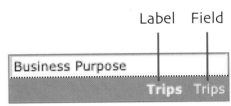

8 Save the Layout by choosing Layouts > Save Layout. Or you can switch to another mode (such as Preview) and save changes when prompted to do so.

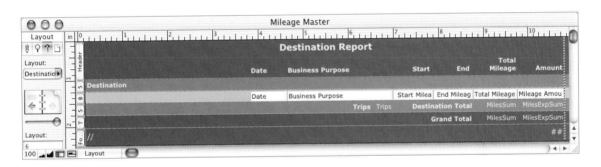

The completed layout (Layout mode).

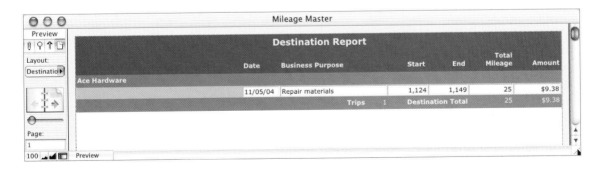

The completed layout (Preview mode).

creating the destination report

extra bits

group by destination p. 85

- Replacing a field rather than deleting the original and dragging a new field onto the layout has the advantage of retaining the original field's formatting.

- When setting the width of the Destination field, the object is to give it sufficient space so that long destinations aren't truncated.

create a trip count field p. 88

- The Trips field could actually be a count of almost any field in the Body part of the layout, such as Business Purpose or End Mileage.

- For the Destination Report to display properly, you'll have to sort the data. Choose Records > Sort Records, and sort on Destination and Start Mileage.

8. adding buttons, scripts, and value lists

Automation in FileMaker Pro is accomplished via scripts. Scripts are created in a part of FileMaker called ScriptMaker and consist of steps (instructions) that FileMaker executes in sequence. A script can perform a one-step operation, such as switching to a particular layout, or it can contain a complex series of steps, such as selecting a subset of records, sorting them, switching to a report layout, displaying and printing the resulting report, re-sorting the records to their original order, and then returning to the original layout.

There are several ways you can execute a script. First, any script can be listed in the Scripts menu, where it can be chosen in the same way that you choose other menu commands. The first ten listed scripts are assigned a ⌘ (Mac) or Ctrl (PC) keyboard shortcut numbered from 1 through 0. Second, you can attach a script to a graphic button on any layout. Clicking the button executes its script.

In this chapter, we'll create the scripts needed to automate a variety of useful functions in the Mileage Master database, such as creating and deleting records, switching layouts, and generating reports. In the process, you'll get a thorough introduction to ScriptMaker. You'll also learn about creating and using value lists. A value list is a list of data values than can be attached to a field to make data entry easier and ensure consistency.

create a button

We'll start by creating the simplest script in the database. It will be attached to a button that takes you from the Global Settings layout back to the Data Entry layout. Switching layouts by clicking a button is more natural and convenient than choosing the layout from the layouts menu. Because the script has only one step and will be attached to a button, it can be created without using ScriptMaker.

1 Switch to Layout mode (View > Layout Mode) and select the Global Settings layout from the layouts pop-up menu.

Button Tool

2 Click the Button Tool. Drag a long button centered beneath the Global Settings text. When you release the mouse button, the Specify Button dialog box appears.

Global Settings

Drawing the button outline

3 Select Go to Layout as the script step, choose Data Entry as the destination layout (in the Options section), and then click OK. A blinking cursor appears in the center of the blank button, waiting for you to type its label.

Step options

Selected step

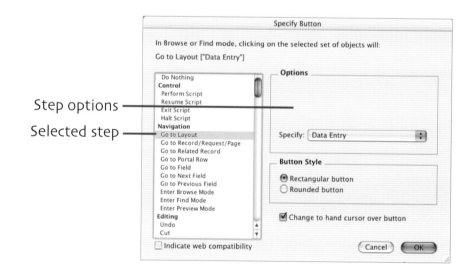

4 Type Return to Data Entry as the button's label. Click away from the button to finalize the text.

5 You can optionally select a new button color from the Fill Color palette, as well as change the format of the button text by selecting font settings from the Text Formatting toolbar. Make any desired changes.

6 To test the button, switch to Browse mode (View > Browse Mode) and click the button. The Data Entry screen should appear.

add Data Entry buttons

It's time to fill that gap at the top of the Data Entry layout. In the Icons folder of the material you downloaded from my Web site are graphic buttons that you'll place at the top of the layout. After you place the buttons, you'll create a script to attach to each button.

1 Switch to Layout mode and choose the Data Entry layout from the layouts pop-up menu.

2 Choose Insert > Picture. In the Insert Picture dialog box, navigate to the drive and folder where you extracted the downloaded material. Open the Icons folder, select New.tif, and click Open.

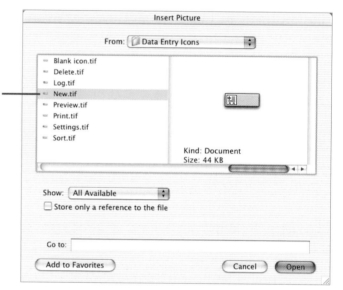

3 Drag the icon to the upper-left position above the layout. Using the arrow keys or the Size palette, align the icon's left side with the left edges of the items below it.

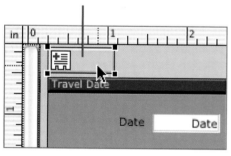

Settings.tif

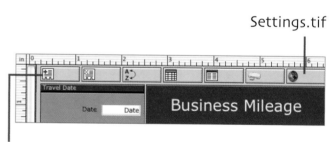

4 Repeat this procedure to place these remaining icons in a line across the top: Delete.tif, Sort.tif, Log.tif, Preview.tif, Print.tif, Settings.tif. Nudge them into position, spacing them as shown. Align the right edge of the Settings icon with the right edge of the Business Mileage title block below it.

label the buttons

The icons on the buttons are purposely small in order to provide room for text labels.

1 Select the Text Tool, click the first icon to set the insertion point, and set the font to something small (such as Arial 8 or 9 pt., black). Type New, press [Shift][Return] to insert a line break, and then type Record. Click away from the text to complete the label.

2 Nudge the selected label into position. If necessary, reduce the width of the text block to ensure that it fits within the bounds of the label.

3 Copy/Paste or Duplicate the text block, move the copy into position on the next label, and edit the text. Repeat for the remaining labels. The labels should read Delete Record, Sort, Trip Log, Mileage Report, Print Report, and Settings.

4 When the labels are in their final positions, you can group each one with its respective icon to prevent the label from inadvertently moving. [Shift]-click an icon and its label, and choose Arrange > Group ([⌘][R]/[Ctrl][R]).

create one-step scripts

We'll create two simple button scripts first—ones that consist of only a single step and that can be completely defined in the Specify Button dialog box.

1 The purpose of the Delete Record button is to delete the current record. Select the Delete Record button on the Data Entry layout and choose Format > Button. In the Specify Button dialog box, scroll down to the Records section of the step list. Select the Delete Record/Request step, do not check the Perform without dialog option, and then click OK. FileMaker attaches the one-step script to the button.

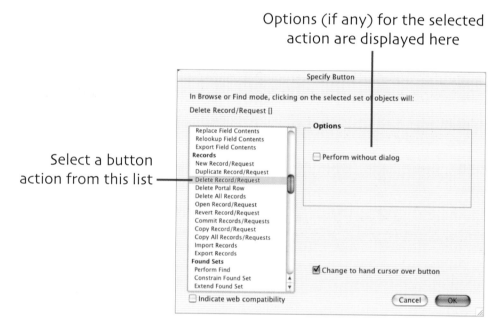

Options (if any) for the selected action are displayed here

Select a button action from this list

2 The Settings button switches you to the Global Settings layout. Select the Settings button on the Data Entry layout and choose Format > Button. In the Specify Button dialog box, select the Go to Layout step, choose Global Settings from the Specify drop-down menu, and click OK.

adding buttons, scripts, and value lists

create the sort script

The Sort Records script is used to arrange the records in Start Mileage order—the order in which the trips occurred. While a sort of the current found set (displayed data) can be created entirely within the Specify Button dialog box, there are additional actions that we also want to perform. Because the script contains multiple steps, it must be created in ScriptMaker.

1 Choose Scripts > ScriptMaker. Because this is the database's first script, the Define Scripts dialog box is empty. Make sure that Include in menu is checked, and then click New.

2 In the Edit Script dialog box, name the script by entering Sort Records in the Script Name text box.

3 The first script step is Show All Records. Issuing the Show All Records command ensures that the entire database is visible (in case you recently performed a Find and are working with only a subset of the records). To add this step to the script, scroll down to the Found Sets section of the step list, select Show All Records, and click the Move button.

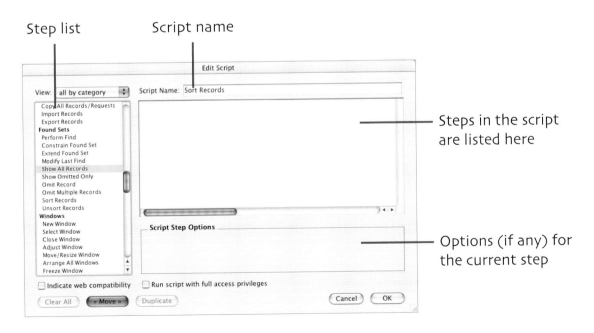

Step list

Script name

Steps in the script are listed here

Options (if any) for the current step

4 The next script step you'll add is Sort Records. Move the Sort Records step from the Found Sets section of the step list. Click the Perform without dialog check box, and then click the Specify button to set the sort instructions. The Sort Records dialog box appears. Double-click the Start Mileage field to add it to the Sort Order list (if it isn't already present), and then click OK to dismiss the dialog box.

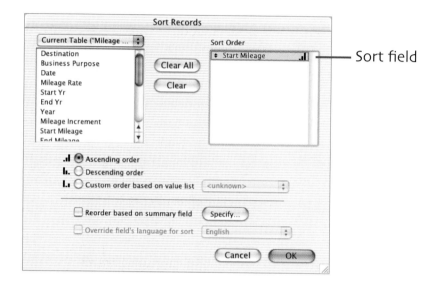

Sort field

5 The final step is to display the last (most recent) record in the database. (Normally, the first record in the current sort order is displayed following a sort.) From the Navigation section of the step list, add the Go to Record/Request/Page step. Choose Last from the Specify pop-up menu.

6 Click OK to complete the script. Click OK again to dismiss ScriptMaker.

```
⇵  Show All Records
⇵  Sort Records [Restore; No dialog]
⇵  Go to Record/Request/Page [Last]
```

Steps and options for the Sort Records script

7 Select the Sort button on the layout and choose Format > Button. In the Specify Button dialog box, select Perform Script as the step, click the Specify button, select the Sort Records script, and click OK. Click OK again to dismiss the dialog box.

create the trip log script

When you need additional trip log forms, this script will print a year's supply (three copies, four per page).

1 Choose Scripts > ScriptMaker. Leave Include in menu checked (so the script will also be listed in the Scripts menu), and then click New.

2 In the Edit Script dialog box, name the script Print Blank Forms.

3 The first step is to enter Browse mode. (This step is frequently issued to ensure that the correct mode is in effect while a script runs.) Add the Enter Browse Mode step from the Navigation section of the step list. Set no options for the step.

4 Next, we'll display the layout that we want to print. Add the Go to Layout step from the Navigation section of the step list. Choose Blank Forms from the Specify pop-up menu.

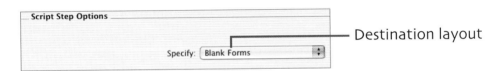

Destination layout

5 To ensure that the Page Setup settings are correct, we'll add a Page/Print Setup command. In the Files section of the step list, select Print Setup and move it into the script. In the Script Step Options area, click Perform without dialog. Then click the Specify button. The Page/Print Setup dialog box appears.

Make sure that the correct destination printer and paper size are selected, and set portrait mode printing. Click OK to close the dialog box.

Selected printer

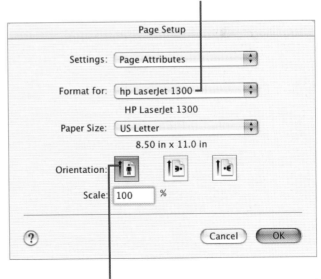

Portrait icon   Macintosh dialog box

adding buttons, scripts, and value lists

create the trip log script

6 Now we'll add the command to print the form. In the Files section of the step list, select the Print step and move it into the script. In the Script Step Options area, click Perform without dialog and then click the Specify button. The Print dialog box appears.

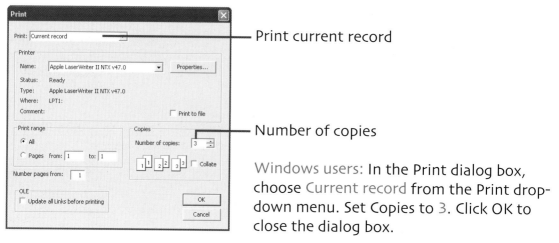

Print current record

Number of copies

Windows users: In the Print dialog box, choose Current record from the Print drop-down menu. Set Copies to 3. Click OK to close the dialog box.

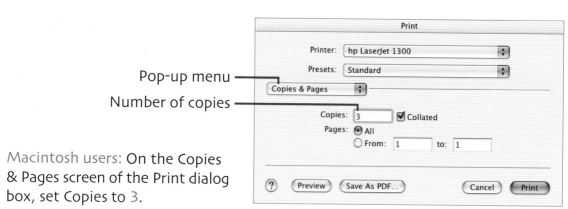

Pop-up menu

Number of copies

Macintosh users: On the Copies & Pages screen of the Print dialog box, set Copies to 3.

adding buttons, scripts, and value lists

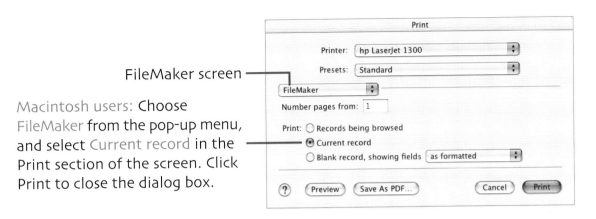

FileMaker screen

Macintosh users: Choose FileMaker from the pop-up menu, and select Current record in the Print section of the screen. Click Print to close the dialog box.

7 The final step is to return to the Data Entry layout. From the Navigation section of the step list, add the Go to Layout step to the script. Choose Data Entry from the Specify pop-up menu.

```
‡  Enter Browse Mode []
‡  Go to Layout ["Blank Forms"]
‡  Print Setup [Restore; No dialog]
‡  Print [Restore; No dialog]
‡  Go to Layout ["Data Entry"]
```

The Print Blank Forms script

8 To save the script, click OK. Click OK again to exit ScriptMaker.

9 Switch to Layout mode, select the Trip Log button on the layout, and choose Format > Button. In the Specify Button dialog box, select Perform Script, click the Specify button, select the Print Blank Forms script, and click OK. Click OK again to dismiss the dialog box.

create new record script

Normally, you create a new record by pressing ⌘N/Ctrl N. In Mileage Master, however, the New Record script also fills in the Start Mileage field by copying and pasting the End Mileage data from the previous record, and then uses your Mileage Increment number to set the End Mileage field. (Even if you've done some personal driving since the last business trip, it's usually quicker to edit these mileage numbers than to enter them manually.)

1 Create a new ScriptMaker script. Name it New Record.

2 From the Found Sets section of the step list, move the Show All Records step into the script. This step ensures that you're working with all records in the database, rather than a subset.

3 Move the Sort Records step from the Found Sets section into the script. Click Perform without dialog, and then click the Specify button to set the sort instructions. In the Sort Records dialog box (see page 98), set Start Mileage as the sort field. Click OK to close the Sort Records dialog box.

4 From the Navigation section, move the Go to Record/Request/Page step into the script. Choose Last from the Specify pop-up menu. When executed, this step will display the last record in the database (in the current sort order).

5 From the Editing section of the step list, add the Copy step. Check the Select entire contents check box, and then click the Specify button. In the Specify Field dialog box that appears, select End Mileage and click OK.

6 From the Records section of the step list, add the New Record/Request step.

7 From the Editing section, add the Paste step. In the Script Step Options area, check Select entire contents, and click the Specify button. In the Specify Field dialog box, select Start Mileage as the field in which to paste and then click OK.

Select the field in which to paste

8 From the Fields section of the step list, add the Insert Calculated Result step. Leave Select entire contents checked. (Doing so ensures that if data is already in the End Mileage field, it will all be replaced with the incremented data.)

9 Click the Go to target field check box to select the field in which the calculated result will appear. In the Specify Field dialog box, select End Mileage and then click OK.

10 Click the Specify button to the right of Calculated result to create the formula. In the Specify Calculation dialog box, create the formula by double-clicking the Start Mileage field, clicking the plus (+) button, and then double-clicking the Mileage Increment field. Here's how the formula should look:

Mileage Master::Start Mileage + Mileage Master::Mileage Increment

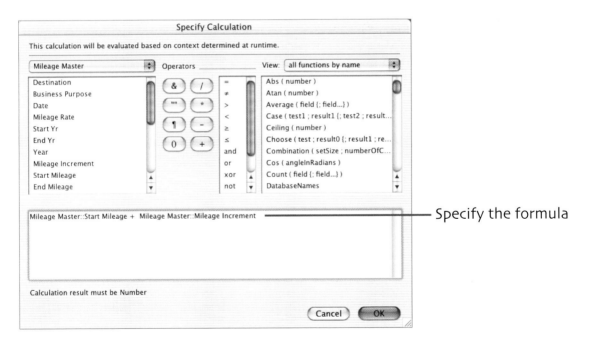

Specify the formula

11 Click OK to close the Specify Calculation dialog box.

create new record script

12 The last step of the script will position the cursor in the Date field in preparation for entering data. From the Navigation section of the step list, add the Go to Field step. Click the Specify button. Select Date in the Specify Field dialog box and click OK. Close the ScriptMaker dialog boxes by clicking OK twice.

```
‡  Show All Records
‡  Sort Records [Restore; No dialog]
‡  Go to Record/Request/Page [Last]
‡  Copy [Select; Mileage Master::End Mileage]
‡  New Record/Request
‡  Paste [Select; Mileage Master::Start Mileage]
‡  Insert Calculated Result [Select; Mileage Master::End Mileage; Mileage Master::Start Mileage +  Mileage Master::Mileage Increment]
‡  Go to Field [Mileage Master::Date]
```

13 In Layout mode, select the New Record button and choose Format > Button. In the Specify Button dialog box, select Perform Script, click Specify, select the New Record script, and click OK. Click OK to close the Specify Button dialog box. The script is now attached to the New Record button.

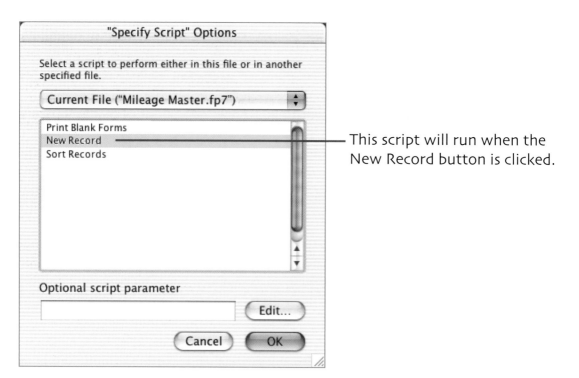

This script will run when the New Record button is clicked.

adding buttons, scripts, and value lists

define value lists

A value list is a list of data values that you can link to a field. The most common use for a value list is to provide a series of choices for the user, formatted as a drop-down list, menu, radio buttons, or check boxes. Value list examples include yes and no, a list of accepted credit cards or shipping methods, and the days of the week. Mileage Master uses three value lists which we'll create: Months, Destination, and Purpose.

Months value list. At present, sorting by the Months field when preparing the Mileage Report results in the trip data being correctly grouped by month, but in alphabetical order. By creating a Months value list of month names in calendar order, we can use it to arrange the data in the proper order.

1 Choose File > Define > Value Lists. In the Define Value Lists dialog box, click New. The Edit Value List dialog box appears.

2 Type Months in the Value List Name box.

3 Select the Use custom values radio button. Enter the months of the year, pressing [Return] (Mac) or [Enter] (PC) after each month name except the last one. Then click OK to return to the Define Value Lists dialog box.

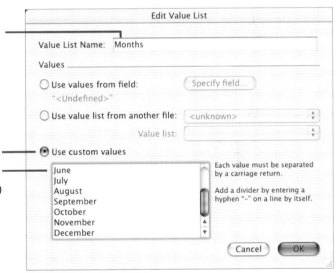

FileMaker won't sort a custom value list for you. You must enter it in the order in which you want it to be presented.

define value lists (cont.)

Value lists from field data. A second method of creating a value list is to base it on the contents of a particular field. When you don't have a preset list of data values, this is an excellent way to effortlessly generate the list. Whenever you enter a new value for the selected field, it is automatically added to the value list. As a bonus, the list is always kept sorted.

1 To create the Destination value list, choose File > Define > Value Lists. In the Define Value Lists dialog box, click New. The Edit Value List dialog box appears.

2 Type Destination in the Value List Name text box.

3 Click the Use values from field radio button. The Specify Fields for Value List dialog box automatically appears.

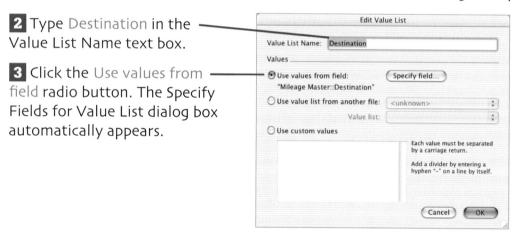

4 To view the field list, choose Mileage Master from the pop-up menu.

5 Select the Destination field, and click OK to return to the Edit Value List dialog box.

6 Click OK again to complete the value list definition and return to the Define Value Lists dialog box.

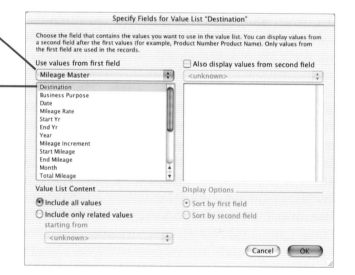

adding buttons, scripts, and value lists

7 Switch to Layout mode. Select the Destination field on the Data Entry layout, and choose Format > Field Format. The Field Format dialog box appears.

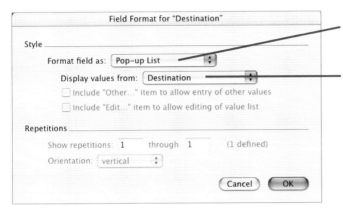

8 Choose Pop-up List from the Format field as pop-up menu.

9 Choose Destination from the Display values from pop-up menu. Then click OK to return to the layout.

10 Repeat these steps to define the Business Purpose value list, based on and linked to the Business Purpose field.

When you're done, the Define Value Lists dialog box will look like this.

11 If you've already created some sample records, you can try out the two value lists by switching to Browse mode and tabbing into the Destination and Business Purpose fields on the Data Entry layout.

When you tab into the Destination field, its value list pops up. Click to select an item from the list or type a new destination name.

create report scripts

There will be two versions of the Mileage Report and the Destination Report: one for viewing onscreen and another to be printed. All four reports can be chosen from the Scripts menu. The two Mileage Report versions can also be run by clicking buttons on the Data Entry layout.

Mileage Report - Screen. This script generates the onscreen version of the report.

1 Choose Scripts > ScriptMaker. Leave Include in menu checked (so the script will also be listed in the Scripts menu), and then click New.

2 In the Edit Script dialog box, name the script Mileage Report - Screen.

3 Add the Enter Browse Mode step from the Navigation section of the step list.

4 Add the Go to Layout step from the Navigation section of the step list. Choose Mileage Report from the Specify pop-up menu.

5 This is a landscape mode report. Add the Print Setup step from the Files section, check Perform with dialog, click the Specify button, set landscape printing in the Page Setup/Print Setup dialog box (see page 99), and click OK.

6 From the Windows section of the step list, add the Adjust Window step. Choose Maximize from the Specify pop-up menu.

7 Add the Sort Records step from the Found Sets section, check Perform without dialog, and click Specify. In the Sort Records dialog box, select Month and Start Mileage as the sort fields.

8 Select Month in the Sort Order list, click the Custom order based on value list radio button, and choose Months from the pop-up menu. Click OK to dismiss the dialog box.

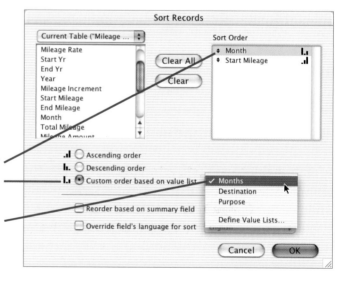

9 Add the Enter Preview Mode step from the Navigation section of the step list. Click the Pause check box. (This will enable you to flip through the pages of the report by clicking the Book icon.)

10 Add the Enter Browse Mode step from the Navigation section of the step list.

11 Add the Go to Layout step from the Navigation section of the step list. Choose Data Entry from the Specify pop-up menu.

12 Add the Adjust Window step from the Windows section of the step list, and choose Restore from the Specify pop-up menu. (Restore makes the window revert to its previous size.)

13 From the Found Sets section of the step list, add the Sort Records step. Check Perform without dialog, and click the Specify button. In the Sort Records dialog box, set Start Mileage as the sort field. Click OK to dismiss the dialog box.

14 Add the Go to Record/Request/Page step from the Navigation section of the step list, and choose Last from the Specify pop-up menu. This step will cause the last record in the database (in the current sort order) to be displayed.

15 Click OK to close the Edit Script dialog box, and then click OK to close the Define Scripts dialog box.

```
✦ Enter Browse Mode []
✦ Go to Layout ["Mileage Report"]
✦ Print Setup [Restore; No dialog]
✦ Adjust Window [Maximize]
✦ Sort Records [Restore; No dialog]
✦ Enter Preview Mode [Pause]
✦ Enter Browse Mode []
✦ Go to Layout ["Data Entry"]
✦ Adjust Window [Restore]
✦ Sort Records [Restore; No dialog]
✦ Go to Record/Request/Page [Last]
```

The Mileage Report - Screen script

16 To link the script to its button, switch to Layout mode, display the Data Entry layout, select the Mileage Report button, and choose Format > Button. In the Specify Button dialog box, select Perform Script, click Specify, select the Mileage Report - Screen script, and click OK. Click OK again to dismiss the dialog box.

create report scripts (cont.)

Mileage Report - Printer. Because this script is simply a variation of the previous one, we'll duplicate the Mileage Report - Screen script, but substitute a Print step for the Enter Preview Mode step.

1 Choose Scripts > ScriptMaker. In the Define Scripts dialog box, select the Mileage Report - Screen script, and click the Duplicate button. Select the Mileage Report - Screen Copy script, leave Include in menu checked, and click Edit.

2 In the Edit Script dialog box, change the script name to Mileage Report - Printer.

3 In the script, select the Enter Preview Mode step and the Enter Browse Mode step below it. Click the Clear button to delete these steps.

4 Select the first Sort Records step in the script. From the Files section of the step list, add the Print step to the script. It should appear immediately below the Sort Records step. Check Perform without dialog. Click the Specify button and set the following options in the Print dialog box (see pages 100–101):

Macintosh users: On the Copies & Pages screen, ensure that the correct printer is selected and that Copies is set to 1. On the FileMaker screen, select Records being browsed. Click Print to close the dialog box.

Windows users: Ensure that the correct printer is selected. Choose Records being browsed from the Print drop-down menu, set Copies to 1, and click OK to close the dialog box.

5 Click OK to close the Edit Script dialog box, and then click OK to close the Define Scripts dialog box.

6 In Layout mode, display the Data Entry layout, select the Print Report button, and choose Format > Button. In the Specify Button dialog box, select Perform Script, click Specify, select the Mileage Report - Printer script, and click OK. Click OK again to dismiss the dialog box.

```
‡  Enter Browse Mode []
‡  Go to Layout ["Mileage Report"]
‡  Print Setup [Restore; No dialog]
‡  Adjust Window [Maximize]
‡  Sort Records [Restore; No dialog]
‡  Print [Restore; No dialog]
‡  Go to Layout ["Data Entry"]
‡  Adjust Window [Restore]
‡  Sort Records [Restore; No dialog]
‡  Go to Record/Request/Page [Last]
```

Destination Report - Screen. The Destination report is a variation of the Mileage Report that organizes the data according to destination instead of month. As such, its scripts are also very similar to the Mileage Report scripts. Rather than creating the Destination scripts one step at a time, we'll duplicate the Mileage Report scripts and then make the necessary changes.

1 Choose Scripts > ScriptMaker. In the Define Scripts dialog box, select the Mileage Report - Screen script and click the Duplicate button. Select the Mileage Report - Screen Copy script, leave Include in menu checked, and click Edit.

2 In the Edit Script dialog box, change the script name to Destination Report - Screen.

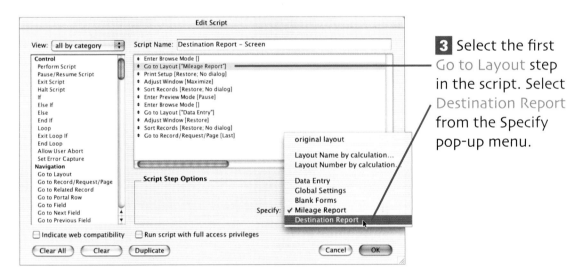

3 Select the first Go to Layout step in the script. Select Destination Report from the Specify pop-up menu.

4 In the script, select the first Sort Records step and click the Specify button. The Sort Records dialog box appears. In order, specify Destination and Start Mileage as the sort fields, and ensure that Ascending order is set for both fields. Click OK to close the Sort Records dialog box.

5 Click OK to close the Edit Script dialog box, and then click OK to close the Define Scripts dialog box.

adding buttons, scripts, and value lists   **111**

create report scripts (cont.)

Destination Report - Printer. The Destination report is for your personal use; that is, the IRS has no interest in its information. Although it's simple to review the report onscreen (using the Destination Report - Screen script), a printing script is provided here for the sake of completeness.

1 Choose Scripts > ScriptMaker. In the Define Scripts dialog box, select the Destination Report - Screen script and click the Duplicate button. Select the Destination Report - Screen Copy script, leave Include in menu checked, and click Edit.

2 In the Edit Script dialog box, change the name to Destination Report - Printer.

3 In the script, select the Enter Preview Mode step and the Enter Browse Mode step below it. Click the Clear button. Then select the first Sort Records step in the script.

```
✦ Enter Browse Mode []
✦ Go to Layout ["Destination Report"]
✦ Print Setup [Restore; No dialog]
✦ Adjust Window [Maximize]
✦ Sort Records [Restore; No dialog]
✦ Enter Preview Mode [Pause]
✦ Enter Browse Mode []
```

4 From the Files section of the step list, add the Print step to the script. Click the Perform without dialog check box. Click the Specify button and set these options in the Print dialog box (see pages 100–101):

Macintosh users: On the Copies & Pages screen, ensure that the correct printer is selected and that Copies is set to 1. On the FileMaker screen, select Records being browsed. Click Print to close the dialog box.

Windows users: Ensure that the correct printer is selected. Choose Records being browsed from the Print drop-down menu, set Copies to 1, and click OK to close the dialog box.

5 Click OK to close the Edit Script dialog box, and then click OK to close the Define Scripts dialog box.

```
✦ Enter Browse Mode []
✦ Go to Layout ["Destination Report"]
✦ Print Setup [Restore; No dialog]
✦ Adjust Window [Maximize]
✦ Sort Records [Restore; No dialog]
✦ Print [Restore; No dialog]
✦ Go to Layout ["Data Entry"]
✦ Adjust Window [Restore]
✦ Sort Records [Restore; No dialog]
✦ Go to Record/Request/Page [Last]
```

The Destination Report - Printer script

make a startup script

We'll create one more script for the database. FileMaker allows you to create two special scripts: a startup and a shutdown script. The former runs automatically whenever you open the database; the latter runs each time you close it. The purpose of both scripts is the same—to prepare the database and put it into a specific state in preparation for this or the next use. The startup script for this database switches to Browse mode, displays the Data Entry layout, ensures that all records in the database are visible and in the correct sort order, and then displays the most recently created record.

1 Choose Scripts > ScriptMaker. Remove the check mark from Include in menu and then click New.

2 In the Edit Script dialog box, name the script Startup.

3 Add Enter Browse Mode (from the Navigation section of the step list) as the first step.

4 Add Go to Layout (from the Navigation section of the step list) as the next step. Choose Data Entry from the Specify pop-up menu.

5 Add Set Zoom Level (from the Windows section of the step list) as the next step. From the Specify pop-up menu, select your preferred magnification for this layout, such as 100% or 150%.

6 Add Move/Resize Window (from the Windows section of the step list) as the next step. Click the Specify button in the Script Step Options area. The "Move/Resize Window" Options dialog box appears.

Set the size (in pixels) of the Data Entry window by entering values for Height and Width (see page 119). Click OK to close the dialog box.

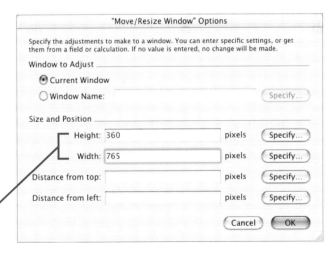

make a startup script

7 To ensure that you're working with all database records rather than a subset, add the Show All Records step (from the Found Sets section of the step list).

8 Add the Sort Records step (from the Found Sets section of the step list). Check Perform without dialog, and click the Specify button. In the Sort Records dialog box, set Start Mileage as the sort field. Click OK to dismiss the dialog box.

9 Add the Go to Record/Request/Page step (from the Navigation section of the step list). Choose Last from the Specify pop-up menu.

10 Click OK to close the Edit Script dialog box. Click OK again to close the Define Scripts dialog box and return to the layout.

> ✦ Enter Browse Mode []
> ✦ Go to Layout ["Data Entry"]
> ✦ Set Zoom Level [150%]
> ✦ Move/Resize Window [Current Window; Height: 360; Width: 765]
> ✦ Show All Records
> ✦ Sort Records [Restore; No dialog]
> ✦ Go to Record/Request/Page [Last]

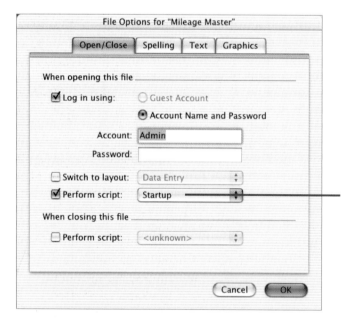

11 Choose File > File Options. On the Open/Close tab of the File Options dialog box, click the Perform script check box and choose Startup from the pop-up menu. Click OK to close the dialog box.

The chosen script will run automatically each time you open the database.

set the script order

Like most user-created lists in FileMaker Pro, you can rearrange the scripts so they're listed in a more logical order in the Define Scripts dialog box and the Scripts menu. Note, too, that all scripts in the Scripts menu are numbered in order of their position in the Define Scripts dialog box.

1 Choose Scripts > ScriptMaker. The Define Scripts dialog box appears, listing all scripts created for the database.

All checked scripts are listed in the Scripts menu. The first ten are assigned keyboard shortcuts.

2 To change a script's placement in the list, click its double arrow and drag it up or down to a new position. Rearrange the scripts to match the order shown here and click OK.

set the script order (cont.)

3 To make it easier to find and choose the desired script from the Scripts menu, you can insert blank lines in the scripts list. To do so, create a new, empty script named - (minus sign). Ensure that the box to the left of the script name is checked. Duplicate the - script twice and position the three in the script list as shown here.

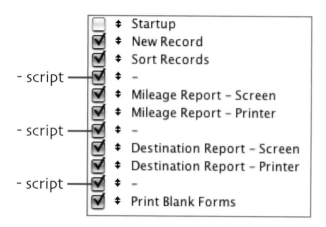

4 Click OK to close the dialog box. The Scripts menu should now look like this.

adding buttons, scripts, and value lists

delete the initial layout

The default layout created when we defined fields is still around. While it doesn't hurt anything to simply leave it, I prefer to eliminate clutter: unnecessary layouts, fields that weren't used, and so on.

1 Switch to Layout mode. Choose the default layout from the layouts pop-up menu. (In FileMaker Pro 7, the default layout has the same name as the database; in this case, Mileage Master. In earlier versions of FileMaker Pro, it's named Layout #1.)

2 Choose Layouts > Delete Layout. Click Delete in the confirmation dialog box that appears.

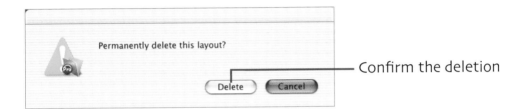

Confirm the deletion

extra bits

create a button p. 92

- When using the Button tool, you can make a rectangular button or one with rounded corners by selecting an option from the Button Style section of the Specify Button dialog box (see page 92).

- You can create a button without immediately associating it with a script or single action. Choose Do Nothing in the Specify Button dialog box. You can set the script or action when you're ready.

add Data Entry buttons p. 94

- When inserting images into a layout or record, check Store only a reference to the file in the Insert Picture dialog box when two conditions exist. First, the images' locations must be constant and accessible to FileMaker Pro. Second, if the original images are huge, storing references to their locations will keep the database from becoming unnecessarily large.

- A Blank icon.tif is included in the icon images. Use it if you want to design your own icons.

- In addition to creating buttons with the Button Tool and importing icons, you can treat virtually any object as a button, such as a text label, for example.

create one-step scripts p. 96

- When creating the action for the Delete button, you'll note that Perform without dialog was not checked. If you're a careful user, you can check this option. Note, however, that you cannot Undo deletions. This is why all Delete commands are normally accompanied by a confirmation dialog box.

create the sort script p. 97

- You can also add a step to a script by double-clicking the step name.

- When creating or editing a script in ScriptMaker, you can delete an unwanted step by selecting it and clicking Clear. To change a step's position in a script, click the double arrow that precedes the step and drag it to a new position.

- The best way to view detailed information about a script is to print it. In the Define Scripts dialog box, select the names of the scripts you want to print and click the Print button.

define value lists p. 105

- When creating a custom value list, the reason you shouldn't leave a blank line at the end of the list is because it will also be treated as a value.

- Value lists can be reused. For example, you can link a Yes/No value list to multiple fields within a database.

make a startup script p. 113

- The dimensions to use when setting a window's height and width will vary from computer to computer—depending on platform and your screen resolution setting. To determine the proper values for your computer, start with the numbers shown in the final script screen shot. Test the value by selecting the Startup script in the Define Scripts dialog box and then clicking Perform. Continue adjusting the values until the window is the desired size.

adding buttons, scripts, and value lists

9. using the database

Now for your reward! You've spent a lot of time creating this database. Now it's finally ready to receive data. This chapter explains how to delete your sample records, enter the Global Settings data, create trip log records, and perform other tasks not covered in the previous chapters. In addition, there are some tips that may give you ideas for ways to customize Mileage Master.

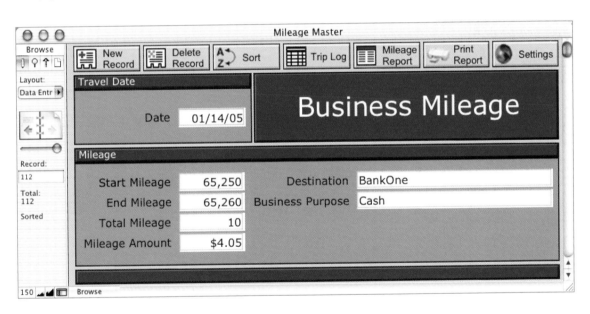

Now that all the pieces are in place, you can start entering data in Mileage Master.

enter the global data

Before you begin entering trip data, there are several important fields that you must fill in on the Global Settings layout.

1 In Browse mode, switch to the Global Settings layout. (Click the Settings button above the Data Entry layout).

2 In the Mileage Rate field, enter the exact value for the IRS-allowable mileage rate for the current year. (Do not enter the dollar sign.)

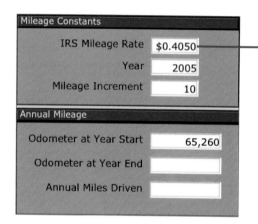

Mileage rate, entered as .405

For 2004, this value was 0.375 (37.5 cents per mile). For 2005, it is 0.405. To find the value in future years, visit www.irs.gov and search for mileage rate.

3 In the Year field, enter the year that this log will cover, such as 2005.

4 In the Mileage Increment field, enter (in miles) the length of your most typical business vehicle trip.

5 In the Start Yr field (Odometer at Year Start), enter the starting odometer reading for the year—presumably from January 1.

Once entered, none of these values should need to be changed during the year. At year-end, enter the final odometer reading in the End Yr field (Odometer at Year End). This number will be used by other fields on this layout to perform calculations.

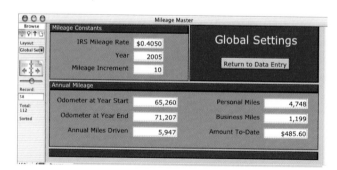

using the database

delete the test records

Now that you've entered the global data, you're ready to begin entering trip data. While you could enter all of a year's data at once, you'll probably find it more palatable to tackle data entry as the year progresses—entering a week or month of trips at a time.

However, assuming that the data you already entered wasn't real data, the first step is to delete all records. (If you have entered real data, you should not perform the following procedure.)

1 Switch to Browse mode and display the Data Entry layout.

2 Check beneath the Book icon to see whether you are currently viewing all records or only a subset. If you're working with a subset, choose Records > Show All Records.

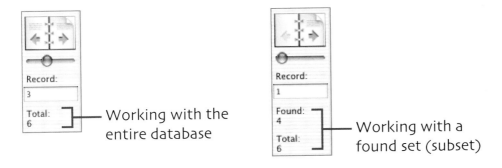

Working with the entire database

Working with a found set (subset)

3 Choose Records > Delete All Records. Click Delete All in the confirmation dialog box that appears. The records are permanently deleted.

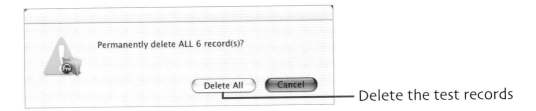

Delete the test records

create the first record

Data entry never really changes, but the first record in Mileage Master is special. Until you've created this record, there is no previous record from which the New Record script can copy data, and the pop-up value lists for Destination and Business Purpose are empty.

1 Ensure that you are in Browse mode and that the Data Entry layout is displayed. Choose Records > New Record or press ⌘N/Ctrl N. Record #1 appears.

2 Because Date is an auto-enter field, today's date automatically appears. Edit the date to match the date of your first trip. Then press Tab to move to the Start Mileage field. (You press Tab to move from field to field.)

3 Enter the odometer reading for the start of the trip.

4 In the End Mileage field, enter the odometer reading at the end of the trip. The total mileage for the trip and its dollar value are calculated.

To simplify things, treat a trip as the total distance traveled; that is, the round trip to and from the specified destination.

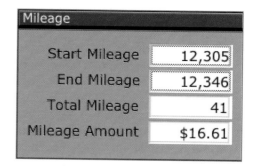

5 When you tab into the Destination and Business Purposes fields, you'll note that a drop-down list does not appear. This is because neither field has an established value list at this point. Typing the first entry in these two fields creates each value list.

6 To complete (commit) the record, press the Enter key on your keyboard's side keypad. (You can also commit the current record by creating a new record, clicking a page on the Book icon to switch to a different record, or changing modes.)

create more records

There a few differences when you create subsequent records (after the first one).

1 Click the New Record button, choose Scripts > New Record, or press the keyboard shortcut assigned to the New Record script. A new record appears.

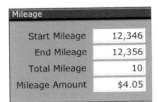

Today's date is inserted into the Date field, Start Mileage is filled with the End Mileage entry from the most recent record, and End Mileage is calculated by adding your Mileage Increment to the Start Mileage figure. Total Mileage and Mileage Amount are also calculated.

2 The cursor appears at the end of the Date field. If the date is incorrect, edit it. Press [Tab] to go to the Start Mileage field.

3 If the Start and End Mileage figures are correct, you can tab through both of them. If either value is incorrect, edit the number. Total Mileage and Mileage Amount are recalculated.

4 When you tab into the Destination field, the field's drop-down value list appears. To select an item from the value list, click the item. To enter a new value (one not in the list), click in the field and type the value. It becomes part of the Destination value list.

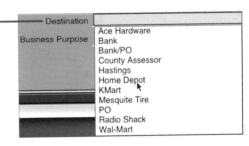

If you select an entry from the list, the cursor automatically moves to the Business Purpose field; if you enter a new value, you must tab into the Business Purpose field.

5 Enter data for the Business Purpose field in the same way that you did for the Destination field.

6 If you have more trips to enter, repeat Steps 1–5 to create each additional record and enter its data. FileMaker automatically saves records as you enter the data.

7 Click the Sort button periodically to put the records in the proper sort order.

using the database

use Data Entry buttons

The buttons above the Data Entry layout serve the same purpose as a toolbar in other programs. That is, they provide convenient access to common procedures (described below). All but the Delete Record and Settings button can also be executed by choosing the appropriate script from the Scripts menu.

New Record. Create a new trip record, automatically filling the fields on the left side of the layout.

Delete Record. Delete the displayed record (after presenting a confirmation dialog box). You can also perform this action by choosing Records > Delete Record or pressing ⌘E/CtrlE. Note that there is no Undo for record deletion commands.

Sort. Sort the records in ascending order by Start Mileage. You only need to sort when the text beneath the Book icon reads Semi-sorted or Unsorted. (Clicking the New Record button performs the same sort, as does running the Startup script.)

Trip Log. Print a year's worth (three pages) of trip log forms. Turn on your printer before clicking this button.

Mileage Report. Display year-to-date trips grouped by month as an onscreen report.

Print Report. Print year-to-date trips grouped by month. Turn on your printer before clicking this button.

Settings. Switch to the Global Settings layout to enter, edit, or view global constants. The Global Settings layout also displays the year-to-date business miles and their dollar value.

find records

If you don't do a lot of business driving, it's relatively simple to locate a given trip record by using the Book icon. Click a page to move one record at a time forward or backward. Or you can drag the slider to jump to an approximate spot in the database or type a record number in the text box.

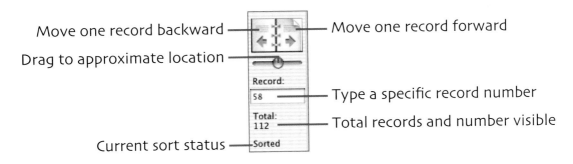

Move one record backward — Move one record forward
Drag to approximate location
Type a specific record number
Total records and number visible
Current sort status

If you have many records, on the other hand, it may be simpler to perform a Find to search for a record or a subset that matches your criteria, such as all trips in which Total Mileage is greater than or equal to 100 miles.

1 With the Data Entry layout displayed, choose View > Find Mode.

2 Enter a criterion in any field on the blank form. To find all trips to a particular location, for example, click the Destination field and select that destination.

3 Click the Find button. Matching records are displayed and all others are temporarily hidden.

4 Use the Book icon to flip through the visible records (called the found set). When you're done viewing the found records, you can click the Sort button to restore the full database.

start a new year

Mileage Master is designed to collect a year's worth of data (January through December). Rather than continuing to use the same database after a calendar year ends, you should print the reports and then create a fresh, blank copy of the database to use for the new year.

1 Choose File > Save a Copy As.

2 In the Create a copy named dialog box, select clone (no records) from the Type (Mac) or Save a (PC) pop-up menu. Select a location for the new file.

3 In the Save As (Mac) or File Name (PC) text box, enter Mileage Master followed by the year (such as Mileage Master 2006.fp7). Click Save.

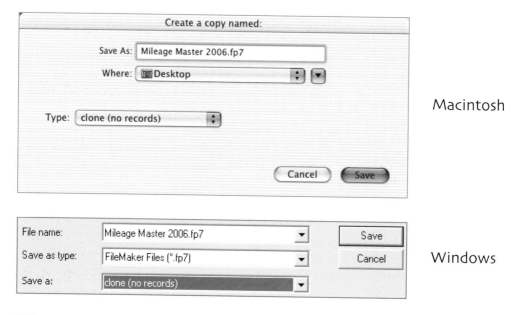

Macintosh

Windows

4 Close the original database and open the clone you just created. Record your trips for the new year in this new copy of the database. Keep the previous year's database for your records.

using the database

customization tips

Database creation is a lot like desktop publishing. There are always so many other features you could add and tiny formatting changes you could make that it's difficult to decide when a database is really finished. Here are some suggestions that you may wish to explore.

Layout changes. There are unlimited tweaks you can make to the Data Entry, Global Settings, and report layouts to make them more attractive. For example, by adding the Emboss effect to headings, you can make them stand out more. You could also add an embossed rectangle around the Data Entry and Global Settings layouts (shown below).

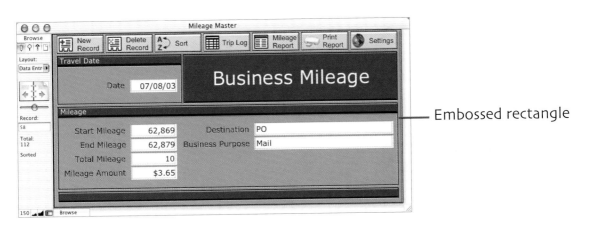

Embossed rectangle

FileMaker Mobile. With a copy of the FileMaker Mobile software installed on your Palm handheld or compatible device, you can dispense with the log forms. You can have a version of Mileage Master installed on your Palm, use it to record your trips while in your vehicle, and then periodically synchronize the Palm's data with Mileage Master on your Mac or PC. For more information on FileMaker Mobile, visit www.filemaker.com.

customization tips (cont.)

Reports without detail. If you don't want to see the actual trips that make up the sections of a report, you can duplicate the report and then delete the Body part. Doing this with a copy of Mileage Report - Screen, for example, will display only the monthly totals.

The revised layout and report below contain neither the Body nor Subsummary (Trailing) parts. I moved the MileSum and MilesExpSum fields up into the Subsummary (Leading) part, made all the text in that part black, and changed the part color to white. If you want to add the same layout to your database, be sure to work on a duplicate of the Mileage Report layout rather than the original.

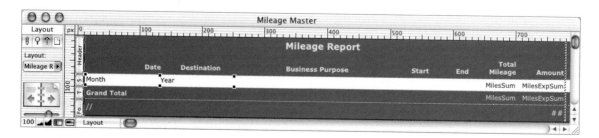

The modified report viewed in Layout mode.

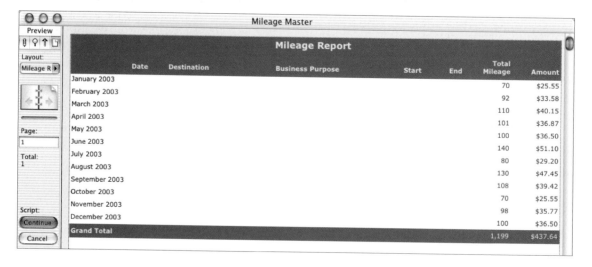

The modified report viewed in Preview mode.

using the database

extra bits

enter the global data p. 122

- When creating the Global Data layout we didn't set a tab order for it. If you'd like to do so (even though it's essentially only a single record in which data isn't entered all at once), see the instructions in Chapter 3.

- Although it probably won't be necessary, it is okay to change the values on the Global Settings layout. Any affected data values in the database will be recalculated.

create more records p. 125

- When working in a pop-up list such as the ones displayed for the Destination and Business Purpose fields, you can also select a value using the keyboard. Press ⬆ or ⬇ to highlight the desired value and press Return/Enter to accept it.

find records p. 127

- You can also set multiple criteria when performing a Find. If you enter the criteria on the same blank form, you are conducting an AND search. Entering "Bank" and "Cash" in the Destination and Business Purpose fields will find only those records that contain both those entries. That is, only records that satisfy all the specified criteria will be displayed.

- You can also sort a database to find records. For instance, if you were looking for a specific lengthy trip, you could perform a descending sort on Total Mileage. Then you'd flip through the sorted records by clicking Book pages.

customization tips p. 129

- If you get a new printer, you should edit the four report scripts so they use the new printer. Margins and other print settings are specific to the printer in use. In ScriptMaker, open each script and select the new printer in the Print and Print Setup steps.

- As you probably gathered, Mileage Master is a single-vehicle database. To track mileage for multiple vehicles, create a copy of the database for each vehicle. (Refer to the instructions in "start a new year.")

index

, (comma) separator, 43, 73
$ (currency symbol), 43
// (Date placeholder), 77, 81
(Page Number
    placeholder), 77, 81
3-D bars, 37
3-D Emboss effect, 82
3-D formatting, 78

a

Align command, 46
Align Right icon, 42, 72
Alignment options, 29, 42,
    54, 55
And search, 8, 131
Annual Dollar field
    adding to layout, 52
    creating, 20
    formatting, 53
    formula for, 16
    label for, 53
    purpose of, 20, 47
Annual Mileage block, 56
Annual Miles field
    copying and pasting, 24
    creating, 20
    formatting, 53
    formula for, 16
    label for, 53
    purpose of, 20, 47
Arrange > Align command,
    46, 58
Arrange > Group command,
    35, 58, 65, 95

Arrange > Send to Back
    command, 39
Arrange > Set Alignment
    command, 46, 55, 58, 82
Arrange > Ungroup
    command, 39
arrow keys, 46
auto-enter options, 9, 12

b

background blocks, 35–36
background graphics, 35, 39,
    49–50. See also graphics
Blank Forms layout, 59–66
    adding text to, 64–65, 66
    creating, 60–63, 66
    illustrated, xiii, 59
    printing, 66
    purpose of, xiii
    setting margins for, 62
Blank Layout option, 46
blankform.tif, 60
blocks, background, 35–36
Body part, 31, 34, 76
Bold icon, 29, 39
Book icon, 123, 124, 126,
    127
borders, field, 78
Browse mode, 6, 45, 57
business mileage database.
    See Mileage Master
    database
Business Purpose field, 33,
    68, 124, 125

Business Purpose value list,
    107
button scripts, 96
Button Tool, 29, 92, 118
buttons
    attaching scripts to, 91,
        104, 118
    creating, 92–93, 118
    labeling, 93, 95
    rounding corners of, 118
    testing, 93

c

calculated values, xi
Calculation fields
    checking result type for,
        23
    copying formulas for, 24
    creating, 17–21
    formulas for specific, 16
    how they work, 1
    purpose of, x, 16
    and tab order, 44
calculations. See also
    Calculation fields;
    formulas
    across records, 16
    built-in functions for, 3
    entering constants for, 47
    indexing, 17
    within records, 16
    storing results of, 17
centimeters, measuring in,
    46

index

cloning databases, 128
colors
  field, 39
  fill, 34, 36
  font, 29, 38
  label, 39
  part, 75–77
Color(s) dialog box, 75, 76, 82
Columnar list/report type, 68
comma separator, 43, 73
computer databases, 1. See also databases
constants, xi, 47
Copy command, 66
copying and pasting
  databases, 128
  formulas, 24
  text, 66
Create a Script for This Report screen, 71
currency notation, 43, 73
currency symbol, 43
Current Fill icon, 34
custom colors, 75–77
custom layouts, 22, 25
Customers table, 5

d

Data Entry buttons, 126
Data Entry layout, 25–46
  adding background blocks to, 35–36
  adding buttons to, 94
  adding color to, 34
  adding divider bars to, 37
  adding section labels to, 41
  adding title to, 38
  aligning fields in, 42
  customizing, 25, 129

  deleting records from, 123
  duplicating, 48
  formatting fields in, 42–43
  illustrated, x, 25
  placing fields/labels in, 39–40, 46
  purpose of, x
  saving changes to, 45, 46
  sections/parts needed for, 31
  setting field widths for, 32–33, 46
  setting tab order for, 44
  using wizard for, 25–28, 46
data validation, 3, 9, 14
database programs, 2, 3, 5
databases
  cloning, 128
  creating, 10, 24
  customizing, 129–130, 131
  default layout for, 22
  defined, 1
  defining fields for, 9–21
  downloading graphics for, xvi
  entering data for, 6, 122–126
  features of, 2–4, 8
  finding records in, 2, 6, 8, 127, 131
  flat-file vs. relational, 5, 8
  generating reports from, 4, 67, 83
  naming, 10, 24
  saving, 10, 24
  sorting, 2, 131
  using scripts with, 3, 8, 91
  validating data in, 3, 9, 14
  ways of using, 1

Date field
  adding to layout, 68
  aligning, 42
  creating, 12
  formatting, 42, 72
  purpose of, 12
  setting width of, 32–33
Date placeholder, 77, 81
date symbol, 71
dates, report, 70
decimal format, 43, 73
default layout, 22
Define Database command, 24
Define Database dialog box, x, 10, 88
Define Scripts dialog box, 97, 111, 115, 118
Define Value Lists dialog box, 105, 106
Delete All Records command, 123
Delete Layout command, 117
Delete Record button, 96, 126
Delete Record command, 126
Delete.tif, 94
Destination field
  adding to layout, 68
  aligning, 39
  deleting, 86
  generating value list from, 106, 124, 125
  setting width of, 33, 90
  using as sort field, 85
Destination Report, 83–90
  creating, 83, 84
  defining trip count field for, 88–89, 90
  editing title for, 86
  grouping fields in, 85
  illustrated, xii
  naming, 84

index

printing, 112
purpose of, xii
refining layout for, 86–87
replacing fields in, 90
saving layout for, 89
setting field widths in, 90
viewing, 111
Destination Report - Printer
  script, 112
Destination Report - Screen
  script, 111
Destination value list,
  106–107
divider bars, 37
drawing tools, 60
Duplicate command, 37, 41,
  51, 65, 73
Duplicate Layout command,
  48, 84

e

Edit > Copy command, 66
Edit > Duplicate command,
  37, 41, 51, 65, 73
Edit > Paste command, 66
Edit > Select All command,
  35, 65
Edit > Undo command, 46
Edit Script dialog box, 97, 99,
  108, 110, 111
Edit Value List dialog box,
  106
Emboss effect, 82, 129
End Mileage field
  adding to layout, 68
  aligning, 42
  creating, 14
  entering data for, 124
  formatting, 43, 73
  purpose of, 14, 47
  setting width of, 32–33

and Total Mileage
  formula, 17
  validating, 15
End Yr field, 13, 53, 122
extra bits sections, xv

f

Field Borders dialog box, 78
field definitions, 11
field labels
  arranging/aligning, 55–56
  deleting, 51
  editing, 79
  formatting, 53
  placing, 39–40
  selecting, 39
  setting color of, 39
field list, 10, 23, 24
Field Name box, 11
field types, x, 11
field widths
  for Destination field, 90
  experimenting with, 46
  for Global Settings layout,
    53
  for Mileage Report layout,
    80–81
  techniques for setting,
    32–33
fields
  aligning, 40, 42, 46, 54,
    72
  arranging, 55–56, 58, 82
  calculated (See Calculation
    fields)
  defined, 1
  defining, x, 9–21, 24
  deleting, 90
  duplicating, 51
  entering data into, 1
  formatting, 24, 42–43
  grouping labels with, 58

naming/renaming, 24
positioning, 39–40
removing borders from, 78
replacing, 24, 51–52, 58,
  90
resizing, 58, 80–81, 82
reviewing type/options
  for, 23
setting options for, 9, 11
setting tab order for, 44
setting widths for, 32–33,
  46, 53
sorting, 2
specifying type of, x, 9, 24
validating, 3, 9, 14
Fields tab, x
File > Define Database
  command, 24
File > Page Setup command.
  See Page Setup command
File > Print Setup command.
  See Print Setup command
File > Save a Copy As
  command, 128
FileMaker layouts. See
  layouts
FileMaker Mobile, 129
FileMaker Pro
  advanced book on, xvii
  creating scripts in, 91 (See
    also scripts)
  as cross-platform product,
    ix
  mode-oriented nature of,
    6–7
FileMaker Pro 7 Bible, xvii
Fill Color icon, 75, 76
Fill Color palette, 36, 75, 76
Fill Pattern icon, 34, 75
Fill Tools, 29
Find mode, 6
finding records, 2, 6, 8, 127,
  131

index

flat-file databases, 5, 8
Font Color options, 29, 38
Font options, 29, 38, 58
Font Size options, 29, 38
Footer part, 31
footers, 70, 75, 76, 78, 79
Format > Button command, 96, 101, 104
Format > Date command, 72
Format > Font submenu, 58
Format > Number command, 73
Format > Sliding/Printing command, 73
Format menu, 42
Format Painter tool, 82, 89
formulas, 15, 16, 24. See also Calculation fields; functions
found set, 97, 98, 102, 127
.fp5 file extension, 24
.fp7 file extension, 24
functions, 3, 15, 16, 18

g

global fields, 9, 13, 47
Global Settings layout, 47–58
  arranging fields for, 55–56, 58
  changing values for, 131
  creating, 48
  customizing, 129
  editing, 49–50, 53, 54
  entering data for, 122
  formatting labels for, 53
  illustrated, 47, 52, 54
  purpose of, xi, 47
  replacing fields for, 51–52, 58
  saving, 57
  setting field widths for, 53

setting formatting for, 53–54, 58
  setting tab order for, 131
  switching to, 126
grand totals, 70, 82, 87
Graphic Rulers command, 62
graphics
  adding to layouts, 35
  aligning, 46
  centering, 66
  downloading, xvi
  moving to lower layers, 39
  positioning, 39
  resizing, 49, 50
  selecting, 39
grids, snapping objects to, 32
Group command, 35, 58, 65, 95

h

Header and Footer Information screen, 70
Header part, 31, 75, 79
heads, layout, 38

i

icons, designing, 118
inches, measuring in, 46
indexing fields, 9, 11, 14, 17
Insert > Picture command, 63, 94
Insert Field icon, 29, 58
Insert Part icon, 29
Insert Picture dialog box, 118
Invoices table, 5
invoicing database, 5
IRS mileage rate, xi, 47, 122. See also Mileage Rate field
Italic icon, 29

k

key fields, 5
keyboard shortcuts, ix, 91, 115, 125

l

labels. See also field labels
  aligning, 40, 46, 54, 79
  arranging, 55–56
  button, 93, 95
  deleting, 51
  editing, 54, 79
  formatting, 53–54
  grouping with fields, 58
  section, 41
  selecting, 55
Landscape orientation, 72, 82, 108
Layout icon, 26
Layout mode, 7, 26, 29, 45, 68
Layout Mode command, 26
Layout Setup command, 84
layout tools, 29–30, 46
Layout wizard. See New Layout/Report wizard
layouts, 25–66
  adding background blocks to, 35–36
  adding color to, 34
  adding divider bars to, 37
  adding section labels to, 41
  adding titles/heads to, 38
  aligning fields in, 42, 54
  arranging fields/objects in, 30, 55–57, 58, 82
  Blank Forms (See Blank Forms layout)
  correcting errors in, 46

index

creating, 25, 26–28, 48, 60–63, 68–71
Data Entry (See Data Entry layout)
default vs. custom, 22
defined, 7
deleting, 117
deleting records from, 123
duplicating, 48, 130
editing, 49–50, 53, 54, 72–74, 82
formatting fields in, 42–43
Global Settings (See Global Settings layout)
inserting images in, 118
Mileage Report (See Mileage Report)
naming/renaming, 26, 48, 84
removing unneeded parts from, 31, 46
replacing fields in, 51–52, 58
reverting to last saved version of, 46
saving, 45, 57, 66, 82, 89
sections/parts of, 31
selecting fields for, 27
selecting magnification for, 113
selecting themes for, 25, 28
setting field widths for, 32–33, 46, 53
setting formatting for, 53–54, 58
setting tab order for, 44, 131
sizing objects in, 30, 82
switching between, 92
as view into database, 8
viewing, 45, 57, 82

Layouts > Delete Layout command, 117
Layouts > Duplicate Layout command, 48, 84
Layouts > Layout Setup command, 84
Layouts > Part Setup command, 74, 85
Layouts > Save Layout command, 66, 82, 89
Line Spacing options, 29
Line Tool, 29, 60
log forms, 59, 99
Log.tif, 94

m

Macintosh
    custom colors on, 75
    keyboard shortcuts, ix
    synchronizing with Palm, 129
macros, 3
magnification, 29, 66, 113
margins, 62, 131
Maximize command, 108
measurement units, 46
Mileage Amount field
    adding to layout, 68
    aligning, 42
    creating, 17
    formatting, 43, 73
    formula for, 16
    setting width for, 32–33
Mileage Constants block, 56
Mileage Increment field
    arranging, 56
    creating, 13
    entering data for, 122
    formatting, 53
    label for, 53
    purpose of, 47

Mileage Master database
    automating functions in, 91
    Calculation fields for, 16
    cloning, 128
    copying for multiple vehicles, 131
    copying for new year, 128
    creating, 10
    creating records for, 124–125, 131
    customizing, 129–130, 131
    Data Entry layout for, 25 (See also Data Entry layout)
    defining fields for, 11–21
    downloading graphics for, xvi
    entering data for, 122–126
    field types used in, 11
    finding records in, 127, 131
    Global Settings layout for, 47 (See also Global Settings layout)
    reviewing field list for, 23
    Summary fields for, 16
Mileage Rate field
    adding to layout, 51
    arranging, 56
    creating, 13, 20
    entering data for, 122
    formatting, 53
    label for, 53
Mileage Report, 67–82
    changing part colors for, 75–77
    creating, 68–71, 82
    duplicating, 83, 84, 130
    editing, 72–74, 82
    formatting text/fields for, 78–79, 82
    illustrated, 67, 77

index

Mileage Report (continued)
  printing, 108, 110
  resizing fields for, 80–81, 82
  viewing, 108–109
Mileage Report - Printer script, 110
Mileage Report - Screen script, 108–109, 130
Mileage Report button, xi, 126
MilesExpSum field, 16, 19, 69, 70, 73
MilesSum field
  adding to layout, 51
  creating, 19
  formatting, 53, 73
  grand totals for, 70
  label for, 53
  monthly subtotals for, 69
  purpose of, 16, 47
mode-oriented programs, 6
Mode pop-up menu, 6
Mode tabs, 6
Month field
  adding to layout, 68, 82
  creating, 18
  formatting, 73
  formula for, 16
  sorting on, 85
  using as grouping field, 82
monthly totals report, 67–82
  changing part colors for, 75–77
  creating layout for, 68–71, 82
  editing, 72–74, 82
  formatting text/fields for, 78–79, 82
  resizing fields for, 80–81, 82
  viewing, 81, 82
Months value list, 105

n

naming
  databases, 10, 24
  fields, 24
  layouts, 26, 48, 84
New Database dialog box, 10
New Layout/Report wizard, 25–28, 31, 46, 67
New Record button, 104, 125, 126
New Record command, 74, 124
New Record script, 102–104, 124, 125
New.tif, 94
nudging, 39, 46, 56, 94
Number fields, 13–15
  aligning, 42, 72
  creating, 13–14
  formatting, 24, 42, 43, 53–54, 58
  opening Number Format dialog box via, 58
  purpose of, 13
  validating, 14, 15
Number Format command, 58

o

object grids, 32
Object Size command, 33
objects
  coloring, 34
  positioning, 30, 46
  showing edges of, 30
  sizing, 30
  snapping to grid, 32
odometer readings, xi, 47, 122, 124
one-step scripts, 91, 96, 118

Or search, 8
Oval Tool, 29

p

page break indicator, 35, 62, 66
page breaks, 82
Page Number placeholder, 77, 81
page numbers, 70, 71, 73
Page Setup command
  and orientation options, 72, 82
  and page breaks, 82
  and page margins, 62
  and report script, 108
  and trip log script, 99
Palm devices, 129
Paragraph Alignment options, 29, 54
Paragraph Line Spacing options, 29
part colors, 75–77
Part Setup command, 31, 46, 74, 85
Paste command, 66
patterns, fill, 34
PC. See Windows PC
Pen Tools, 29
Personal Miles field, 16, 20, 21, 47, 53
Personal Miles formula, 24
Picture command, 63, 94
pixels, measuring in, 46
pop-up lists, x, 124, 131
Portal Tool, 29
Portrait orientation, 82, 99
Preferences dialog box, 36
Preview mode, 7
Preview Mode command, 65
Preview.tif, 94

index

Print Blank Forms script, 101
Print dialog box, 100
Print Report button, 126
Print Setup command
  and orientation options, 72, 82
  and page breaks, 82
  and page margins, 62
  and report script, 108
  and trip log script, 99
printer settings, 131. See also Page Setup command; Print Setup command
printing
  Blank Forms layout, 66
  Destination Report, 112
  Mileage Report, 108, 110
  scripts, 118
  trip log forms, 126
Print.tif, 94
Products table, 5

r

records
  creating, 6, 74, 102–104, 124–125, 131
  defined, 1
  deleting, 123, 126
  finding, 2, 6, 8, 127, 131
  grouping, 68
  inserting images in, 118
  sorting, 2, 74, 90, 131
  viewing, 6
Records > Delete All Records command, 123
Records > Delete Record command, 126
Records > New Record command, 124
Records > Sort Records command, 90

Rectangle Tool, 29, 36, 60
reference, FileMaker Pro, xvii
relational databases, 5, 8
report scripts, 108–112
report titles, 70, 72, 86
Report wizard. See New Layout/Report wizard
reports, 67–90
  adding headers/footers to, 70
  calculating subtotals/totals in, 69
  components of, 4
  creating, 68–71, 83
  creating scripts for, 71
  customizing, 129, 130
  deleting lines from, 79
  duplicating, 83, 84, 130
  editing, 72–74
  generating from databases, 4, 67
  grouping fields in, 68
  selecting fields for, 68
  selecting themes for, 70
  viewing, 81, 82
Rounded Rectangle Tool, 29
ruler, 62

s

sales tax, calculating, 16
Save a Copy As command, 128
Save Layout command, 66, 82, 89
saving
  databases, 10, 24
  layouts, 45, 57, 66, 82
  scripts, 101
ScriptMaker, 91, 97. See also scripts
scripts, 91–104

adding steps to, 118
attaching to buttons, 91, 104, 118
and database ease-of-use, 8
deleting steps from, 118
executing, 91
keyboard shortcuts for, 91, 115
new record, 102–104, 124, 125
one-step, 91, 96, 118
printing, 118
purpose of, 3, 8, 91
rearranging, 115
report, 108–112
repositioning steps in, 118
saving, 101
shutdown, 113
sort, 97–98
startup, 113–114, 119
trip log, 99–101
ways of using, 91
Scripts menu, xii, 8, 91, 108, 115–116
section labels, 41
Select a Theme screen, 70
Select All command, 35, 65
Selection Tool, 29, 32, 65
Send to Back command, 39
Set Alignment command, 46, 55, 58, 82
Set Tab Order command, 44
Settings button, 96, 126
Settings.tif, 94
shortcuts, keyboard, ix, 91, 115, 125
Show All Records command, 97
Show/Hide Status Area Tool, 29
Show submenu, 30

index

.shutdown scripts, 113
Silicon Wasteland, xvi
Size palette
    and field/label alignment,
        40, 41, 46, 80
    purpose of, 30
    resizing multiple fields
        with, 58
    setting field widths with,
        33
Sliding/Printing command,
    73
Solid Fill icon, 34
solid fill pattern, 75
Sort button, 125, 126
sort fields, 85
Sort order list, 69
Sort Records command, 74,
    90
Sort Records dialog box, 69,
    98
Sort Records script, 97–98
sorting
    alphabetically vs.
        numerically, 13
    purpose of, 2
    selecting fields for, 69
    as technique for finding
        records, 131
    using script for, 97–98
    value lists, 105
Sort.tif, 94
Specify Button dialog box
    attaching scripts to
        buttons in, 96, 101, 104
    Button Style section, 118
    creating buttons in, 92,
        118
Specify Calculation dialog
    box, 103
Specify Field dialog box, 85

Specify Fields screen, New
    Layout/Report, 68
Specify Grand Totals screen,
    New Layout/Report, 70
Specify Subtotals screen,
    New Layout/Report, 69
Start Mileage field
    adding to layout, 68
    aligning, 42
    creating, 14–15
    entering data for, 124
    formatting, 43, 73
    purpose of, 47
    setting width of, 32–33
Start Yr field, 13, 53, 122
startup scripts, 113–114, 119
storage options, field, 9, 11,
    13
StuffIt Deluxe, 63
StuffIt Extractor, 63
Subsummary part, 75, 77,
    78, 85
subtotals, 69, 82
Summary fields
    creating, 19
    for data entry layouts, 16
    grand totals for, 70, 82
    purpose of, 13
    for reports, 16
    subtotals for, 69, 82
System subset (88 colors)
    palette, 36

t

T-Squares lines, 64
T Tool. See Text Tool
Tab key, 124
tab order, setting, 44, 131
tables, for invoicing
    database, 5

text
    aligning, 42
    blending with background
        color, 87
    copying and pasting, 66
    for field labels, 53–54
    formatting, 29, 53–54, 64
    inserting, 64–65
    for layout titles/heads, 38
    selecting/deselecting, 66
Text fields, 11, 24
Text Formatting toolbar, 29,
    38, 42, 53, 64
text labels. See labels
Text Tool
    and field labels, 54
    illustrated, 29
    and layout text strings, 64
    and layout titles, 38, 50
    and section labels, 41
themes, 25, 28, 70, 72
thousands separator, 43, 73
titles
    layout, 38
    report, 70, 72, 86
Total Mileage field
    adding to layout, 68
    aligning, 42
    creating, 17
    formatting, 43, 73
    formula for, 16
    setting width for, 32–33
totals, 70, 82. See also
    subtotals
Trailing Grand Summary part,
    75, 76, 78, 87
transparent backgrounds, 87
trip count field, 88–89
Trip Log button, 126
trip log forms, xiii, 59, 99,
    126
trip log script, 99–101
Trips field, 88–89, 90

index

u

Underline icon, 29
Undo command, 46

v

validating data, 3, 9, 14
validation formula, 15
value lists
  avoiding blank lines in,
    119
  creating, 105–107, 124
  defined, 91, 105
  reusing, 119
  selecting items from, 107,
    125
  sorting, 105
  ways of using, 105
View > Browse Mode
  command, 57
View > Graphic Rulers
  command, 62
View > Layout Mode
  command, 26
View > Preview Mode
  command, 65
View > T-Squares command,
  64
View menu, 30
Visual QuickProject Guides, ix

w

widths, setting field, 32–33,
  46, 53, 80–81
Windows PC
  custom colors on, 76–77
  keyboard shortcuts, ix
  synchronizing with Palm,
    129
WinZip, 63
wizard. See New Layout/
  Report wizard

y

Year field
  arranging, 56
  creating, 13
  deleting, 85
  entering data for, 122
  formatting, 53, 73
  label for, 53
  purpose of, 47

z

zoom level, 56
Zoom Out/In controls, 29, 66
Zoom percentage, 29

Ready to Learn More?

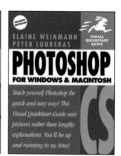

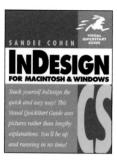

If you enjoyed this project and are ready to learn more, pick up a *Visual QuickStart Guide*, the best-selling, most affordable, most trusted, quick-reference series for computing.

With more than 5.5 million copies in print, *Visual QuickStart Guides* are the industry's best-selling series of affordable, quick-reference guides. This series from Peachpit Press includes more than 200 titles covering the leading applications for digital photography and illustration, digital video and sound editing, Web design and development, business productivity, graphic design, operating systems, and more. Best of all, these books respect your time and intelligence. With tons of well-chosen illustrations and practical, labor-saving tips, they'll have you up to speed on new software fast.

> *" When you need to quickly learn to use a new application or new version of an application, you can't do better than the **Visual QuickStart Guides** from Peachpit Press."*
> Jay Nelson
> *Design Tools Monthly*

www.peachpit.com